My Journey to My Dream

a memoir by
TASOS NIKOPOULOS

Copyright © 2014 by Tasos Nikopoulos
First Edition – August 2014

ISBN
978-1-4602-4276-6 (Hardcover)
978-1-4602-4277-3 (Paperback)
978-1-4602-4278-0 (eBook)

All rights reserved.

No part of this publication may be reproduced in any form, or by any means, electronic or mechanical, including photocopying, recording, or any information browsing, storage, or retrieval system, without permission in writing from the publisher.

Produced by:

FriesenPress
Suite 300 – 852 Fort Street
Victoria, BC, Canada V8W 1H8

www.friesenpress.com

Distributed to the trade by The Ingram Book Company

TABLE OF CONTENTS

Introduction ... 1
Learning How to Dance ... 3
Greek Dancing ... 12
Making Some Changes ... 20
A Taste of Archaeology ... 22
Lots of Dancing ... 25
Competitions ... 38
My Short Trip to Greece ... 43
Cirque du Soleil ... 49
Aerial Silks ... 51
Back to Greece ... 55
Back to the Drawing Board ... 65
Showtime ... 70
Going back to the head office of Cirque du Soleil ... 74
Waiting ... 78
Finally: Dancing with the Stars Greece ... 85
A Surprise ... 91
The Greek Media ... 99
Back Home to Canada ... 102
Florida ... 104
Hard at Work ... 117
Summer 2013 ... 122
Back to Business ... 126
For Real! ... 132
Let's Do it Again! ... 134
It's Not Over, It's Just the Beginning ... 141

Please visit
www.tasosnikopoulos.com
for my resume and audition material.

I dedicate this book to my parents, Harry and Helen Nikopoulos that have been extremely supportive. To my sister, family, friends, cousins, nieces, nephews, godchildren, Canada, Hamilton, Greece and the world! May this book bring you the inspiration to chase your dreams and live life to the fullest.

I also want to dedicate my book to the following inspiring artists and creators.

- Irina Aoucheva — Ballet Dancer, Teacher, Choreographer
- Nilda Comas — Sculptor
- Ruth Offen — Artist
- Eric and Cora Brittan — Artists
- Anthony Manieri — Photographer
- Adriana Salgado Neira and Orlando Reyes Ibarra — Argentine Tango Dancers, Teachers, Choreographers, Show Dancers
- Tanya Cardinal — Ballroom Dancer, Coach, Choreographer, Adjudicator
- Karen Moniz — Come Dancing
- Lou Zamprogna — Director
- Stefano Corapi — Argentine Tango, Ballroom and Latin Dance Instructor and Choreographer
- Bill Stathakos — Computers and Business
- Vasilios Papagianis — Artist
- Dana Vena — Ciao Bella Dance Studio
- Patti Easson, Carm and Connie Sciortino — Social Ballroom Dancers
- Roland Fix and Tom Oliver — Vocal Teachers
- John Ranivand — Dancing at Sea
- Joseph Arevalo — Pianist
- Angelo Tsarouchas — Comedian and Actor
- Nia Vardalos — Actress, Director, Producer, Screenwriter, Singer
- Mark Lany — CROWNS

My Journey to My Dream

INTRODUCTION

I was born March 10th, 1979 in Hamilton, Ontario to immigrant parents that were born and raised in Greece. Since I was a child I had a dream of becoming a ballroom dancer, actor and singer. Dancing came naturally to me and I was in a Greek folklore dance group since I was a child. My chubby little body loved it.

In grade six, I participated in all the plays that were done at my school and as I continued to high school I sang and danced in all of the musical theatre productions. While I was in high school my drama teacher wasn't encouraging to me to further pursue an acting career or I may have misunderstood, but this is how I felt. I wouldn't let this deter me in the future, but at that time I put it on the back burner.

I chose to leave my dream of being a dancer, singer and actor to pursue another: becoming an archaeologist. I furthered my studies at Brock University in St Catharines, Ontario. I first fell in love with archaeology when I was 13 years old while visiting my grandparents and relatives in Greece. I fell in love with the temple of Athena Alea. My grandparents lived close to it, and it's where my mother and aunts grew up.

The temple was in ruins, as all Greek temples were in Greece. Its huge marble foundations were still there; they had gigantic columns that had fallen over and broken into huge pieces. It was the job of the archaeologists to piece them together and try to make sense of something that was in shambles. I went to university and studied and enjoyed archaeology. While I was participating in archaeological excavations, in the back of my mind I was always wondering what it would be like to become a singer, dancer and actor.

Afterward, I went on to Teacher's College, but I never completed the course because I was too busy suffering from a broken heart. My girlfriend left me, she told me she didn't love me anymore and wanted to go on with her life without me. My life fell apart, I needed time to heal and I wanted a change for a while. I decided to go on an adventure.

My ultimate plan was to pursue acting, be on a teacher supply list and work on one archaeology project a year. However, I left Teacher's College and completed enough credits to teach English as a Second Language (ESL) so I opted to teach in South Korea for one year.

I left for South Korea just before my 24th birthday and came back to Canada a year later. I had the time of my life in Korea. I was teaching children and adults, making friends with colleagues and local Koreans.

I visited many places in South Korea and one month before I came home I went on a backpacking adventure. I went to Singapore, Malaysia, Vietnam, Cambodia and ended the trip in Thailand. I made memories that I will cherish for the rest of my life. The trip made me appreciate more of what we had at home in Canada. Some of the places were poor and the people experienced plenty of poverty.

I came home at the end of March, single and ready to chase my dreams. I walked into a franchise dance studio that I had been looking up at for years. Since I was 18 years old, and driving, I would stop at a busy intersection near my home and look up to see people dancing at the franchise dance studio on the second floor of the building. I would always wonder to myself what it would be like to be a dancer.

I went to that studio and the rest is history. I was so excited to have finally found the courage to walk into this place.

LEARNING HOW TO DANCE

MARCH 2005

It was March 25th, 2005 and I had just turned 25 years old. I finally had the guts, after so many years of thinking of dancing, to walk into the dance studio. I walked in and was greeted by the receptionist. I said I was ready and willing to start to learn how to ballroom dance right away.

We took care of the paper work and there was a teacher ready and available to teach me. I was extremely excited gazing at the beautiful hardwood floors and mirrors while people were being taught by dance instructors in the various ballroom and Latin dances.

I was starting to picture myself dancing wearing a long black tuxedo or some hot looking Latin costume. After a minute of daydreaming, I was introduced to my dance instructor. Her name was Anya. She was tall and pretty with dark hair, around my age and of Eastern European descent. She took me into a beautifully decorated office with iron chairs and a white marble table as a desk.

She asked, "Why are you here?"

I replied, "I have a dream. I want to be a ballroom and Latin dancer, a show dancer and a professional competitor. I also want to teach at some point and become a singer and actor too."

We went on to discuss different programs. I learned I could become a teacher and teach at the dance studio. The studio offered dance training to its teachers. I thought, wow, I can teach beginners and learn how to dance at the same time.

We discussed prices and it was going to cost me about $140 a week.

I said, "Wow that's lots of money." I couldn't afford that. I had just come back from South Korea and didn't have a job. The price included one private class a week and unlimited group classes and a dance party on Friday night. I needed time to think about it and figure out how I was going to get the money. Anya did give me a lesson that day, after our conversation.

I went to the bank the next day and got a $7,000 dollar line of credit. I was so happy I called the studio the next day and signed up for dance lessons. I started learning and dancing and proving to my dance instructor how naturally it came to me. In time I met the studio owner. Her name was Shannon. She was a tall woman with short blond hair in her early 40s. She was bubbly, outgoing and a lot of fun.

She observed how well I danced and by May, 2005 I was ready to do my first spotlight dance at the studio. The spotlight dance is when a student dances a routine with his or her instructor and performs it at a Friday night dance party for his or her fellow dance peers. Also, at that time I was ready to do my first pro-am dance competition in the beginner division. The "pro" was my instructor and "am", which means amateur was myself.

It was the first Friday of May and Anya had choreographed a fun and entertaining swing routine. It was full of turns, kicks and tricks. I was feeling a little nervous and excited at the same time. I was going over in my head my routine before I was going to go on the floor to perform. The time was approaching and I was to perform at 8pm. Shannon introduced Anya and me to the crowd and what dance we were going to perform. It was going to be the first time I was going to dance a ballroom style routine in front of a group of people. As I walked on to the dance floor my heart was pounding with excitement.

I said to myself "This is it, give it your best shot."

The music started to play, we started to dance our routine, and the crowd was cheering and applauding as we danced. It was going better than I expected. So far so good. I was enjoying the dance. After about a minute and 20 seconds our routine was coming to an end. It was the last dance trick and it was the most entertaining of all the tricks in the routine. The grand finale. Anya crouched down, I kicked my leg over her head, I pulled her through my legs and up she came, she fell back into my arms and then we crouched down together to the floor and I threw her back up on to her feet again. But the unexpected happened. As Anya was falling into my arms I felt the first seam bust in my pants and as we furthered to the floor I felt the entire seam of my pants burst open like a zipper. This all happened in just under 10 seconds. All of a sudden my forest green underwear was exposed to the crowd through the large opening in the back of my pants. The crowd went silent and stared at me and Anya not knowing how to react. I stared into Anya's eyes and we started to laugh and then the crowd laughed with us too. Here is my advice to a male ballroom dancer: make sure you get ballroom dance pants made if you want to add tricks in a routine and don't use your everyday black dress pants like I did. Traditional dance pants have lycra in them which allows the pants to stretch when doing crouches and tricks. You have much less of a chance of your pants splitting open like mine did. In any case, I enjoyed the routine and now I was ready to do my first pro-am competition which was going to be the following week.

Again, Anya worked hard at choreographing our routines. I practiced as often as I could with her and we were ready for the competition. I had 11 entries during the competition and I won gold and silver medals at the beginner level. I was so excited as I watched the more advanced students with more elaborate routines and I looked forward to the day when I would reach that point in my career too.

Anya and I were sitting at the back of the hall, right in the corner with many tables in front of us. Three huge chandeliers hung above the dance floor and the adjudicators' table was behind the floor. I observed one of the adjudicators, an older gentleman his in 70s, stand up and walk around the large dance floor coming toward me. He said,

"Young man, out of all the competitors today you were the only one who looked like they were having the most fun on the floor the whole day, congratulations!"

He put out his hand for me to shake it and I did.

I said, "Thank you very much sir."

Then he walked away. Anya turned to me in surprise and shock. She explained he was a dinosaur in the dance business and I should be grateful and happy to receive a compliment from him. I didn't have a clue who he was. I was ecstatic and excited that at my first competition I got such a wonderful compliment. Wow, listening to a nice compliment like that drove me to work harder to reach my goal. After that great day I went back to the studio and continued to work hard.

OCTOBER 2005

After dancing for the past seven months and sometimes taking more than one private lesson a week my seven thousand dollars ran out. With a part-time job at our family Greek owned burger joint, I wasn't making enough money to increase my line of credit. I was disappointed and Anya knew I wanted to teach because as an instructor I would get free training.

She spoke with the owner and I got a job as a beginner instructor. I was in the clouds and jumping for joy! I juggled my schedule so I could still help out at the family restaurant and be a dance instructor. This really made me happy. It was so nice to get this job. Now I can work even harder and I could be at the studio everyday learning and teaching new people how to make their dancing come to life too.

I started teaching the end of October, 2005. I remember the first party I was there as an instructor and not as a student. It was the studio's Halloween party. I came dressed up as Zorro in a black mask and cape. All the students were dressed up; some came as maids, a priest and a nun. I was nervous. A woman, a veterinarian named Jill, was a student and she asked me to dance. I told her I was a new instructor. She just danced with me and made me feel like I had been dancing for years. We all had a good time.

I was scheduled to come in and work every day from 2pm until 10pm, from Monday to Friday and I was told that there would be daily training. I heard the word "training" and my heart started to pound because I was so looking forward to learning more and more dance steps, style and technique.

I came in daily as expected for training. At the beginning it was a few times a week and then it started to become less and less — until there was none at all. The studio owner was to conduct the training. However, I learned from this woman (who was fun and outgoing) that she was depressed about certain situations in her life, and as a result, her studio was suffering. She would show up late or not show up at all. I really liked her and felt for her situation, but I was getting frustrated. I begged for training and got it a few times a month. I was so disappointed and I never let anybody know how I felt because I knew she was going through a depressing time.

I was told to take dance manuals and DVDs and teach myself how to dance. Yet having little experience in the dance world to start off with, it was hard and I didn't know where to begin. Looking at these manuals was like reading Japanese upside down. These books had instructions about turns, foot positions and directions. It was basically dance done verbally. It was supposed to be used as a reference and a guide, not as a primary tool for somebody who had no clue about dancing.

As I see it, you learn how to dance from an instructor, not with books and DVDs. They're a great reference and secondary tool, not as a primary tool. If that was the case, why have a studio? I made many, many attempts to try and speak with the owner, but she would change the topic and avoid speaking. One day as I was complaining, yet again, about getting training, she did tell me that a travelling coach was in a nearby city and that she could arrange for her to come to our studio for a day or two.

I said to myself "Finally! I am going to get some dance training"

This coach's name was Mrs. Pat. She was in her 70s and had been in the dance business for over 40 years. She knew her stuff and was extremely strict in her teachings. Everybody was on pins and needles when she was giving coaching sessions; you couldn't get away with murder when she was around even if you tried. Every dance teacher was petrified of her. She didn't want to hear any excuses, cries for help or anything close to it at any time. Everybody addressed her as "Mrs. Pat" all the time. She reminded me of Cruella Deville. She was at our studio on November 12th and 13th. She came into the studio at 11am and trained the staff until 1pm. Afterwards, various students booked her in for a specific time and received dance coaching from her too. She was just as strict.

During one of our teacher training days she was yelling at us every time we made an error, it felt like the army was a walk in the park in comparison to her tactics and when she asked a question she expected to be addressed all the time and anytime as "Mrs. Pat". Well, nobody every addressed her any other way, ever! Except during one of her yelling sessions, when she asked me a question:

"Tasos, as a male in the waltz, do you start the dance with a heel or a toe lead?"

I replied, "Mama Pat, it is with a heel lead."

Everybody and the studio owner stared at me in disbelief of how I had just addressed her. You could see the shock in their faces. I just froze with a nervous smile on my face. I was just testing to see how she would have reacted if I addressed her in a different kind of way. I knew I was pushing my limits. I was curious. Mrs. Pat looked at me with a stone cold look on her face. All of a sudden her reaction was different.

She smiled and said, "Yes little T, that's right"

All the teachers and the studio owner were shocked again because they were probably expecting her to start yelling and she didn't. Mrs. Pat flashed an evil look to the rest of the teachers as if they weren't allowed to call her that. So the rest of the session we continued as "Mama P" and "Little T". Nobody even dared try to call her what I called her. I guess she must have liked the simple fact that I wasn't afraid to challenge her and call her by a different name. I never asked her why. I figured I didn't want to push it. After our coaching sessions were completed, the studio owner went back to not training me.

I was fed up and left at the end of December 2006. I told her how I felt and she understood. I felt bad, but I needed the training that I was promised. She knew how much I wanted to learn how to dance. I said I was sorry and I gave her a hug and she told me that she understood why I was leaving and we left on good terms; I really liked working for her, but I had to leave.

JANUARY 2007

I didn't want to leave the dance business. The thought of leaving the dance world was so upsetting to me. It was a passion of mine and I just didn't want to leave that world. So I looked around to find work at other studios. I found a studio in a nearby city, but they weren't hiring. I went closer to Toronto and found another studio that was hiring dance instructors so I enquired about a position.

I had heard rumours that working for this particular woman was challenging. I thought I would just give it a try. She was described by many people as being difficult and unreasonable. I figured I could handle her. I had met her previously at a dance conference that my old boss had sent me to attend. It was the annual dance convention for instructors. They took place in different cities across North America. This time it was in Los Angeles. These conventions were designed for teacher training purposes. My old boss had paid for me to go and I went because I was always asking for training and she sent me. I had a great time.

This is where I met this new woman, the present studio owner that I had applied to work at for the next while. I slowly discovered that we just didn't see eye to eye on many ideas. I said black she said white. We weren't compatible about views on business and teaching, though, I understood why. She was a strong individual and that's why she had a successful studio. She had a business to run and I wanted to be an artist. It wasn't a good time for me to work with her at her studio.

It was more about business and not the art of dancing. For me, I really wanted to learn how to dance, much more than be a businessman. I wanted to find a professional dance partner and teach and do shows, but I really needed to learn how to dance. Once again I was given dance manuals and DVDs and told to teach myself. I still didn't understand them and tried my best to use the knowledge I had learned. I tried to make sense of these manuals.

She wanted her instructors to be business people not dancers. I knew I could be a good businessman, but I wanted to be a dancer. That was my dream. If I wanted to be a businessman I would have left the dance world and applied to a marketing company of some sort, not a dance studio. I understood that the studios were businesses and they needed to make money and I understood that the owners were there to make money too, but it just seemed to me that nobody cared about the artistic pleasure of dancing.

Before I started dancing for her, I went to Las Vegas with some friends and we went to see "O" by *Cirque du Soleil* and I was so inspired that I wanted to work for this amazing company one day. (I will mention *Cirque du Soleil* again later.)

My new boss and I kept butting heads because the policy was that instructors were to receive dance training and I wasn't getting it. It reminded me of the last dance studio where I worked. I was always the one speaking out at the studios and it seemed nobody else was speaking up. Well, nobody else did and I looked like the impossible employee. I was doing my job and wanted the owner to do her job too.

I discovered this studio was not for me. I learned a lot from my boss even though we didn't see eye to eye. She taught me that staying on top of the business aspect of the studio was important and that's why she had a great business. I left around June which was fine by me because I was going to Greece with our Greek Dance Group. So I would leave my job searching for September.

GREEK DANCING

JULY 2007

It was the beginning of July and we had just under two weeks left before going to Greece with our Greek Dance group, but before I write about my experience in Greece I will write a brief historic timeline of how Greek dancing came into my life.

   I started to learn how to Greek dance at home when I was about four or five years old. My mother loved to dance and loved music so I am certain I inherited it from her. She would move the coffee table in the living room to the side of the room, play music and teach my sister and me how to dance. Also, we learned in Greek school how to dance too. I remember being in Kindergarten at our Greek school at our local Greek community in Hamilton, Ontario learning more Greek dancing steps. Greek school was every Saturday morning from 10am until 1pm. There we learned how to speak, read and write Greek, learned about the geography of Greece and Greek history too. I would have much rather been at home like my non-Greek friends watching cartoons on a Saturday morning. As much as most Greek children dreaded going to school for a sixth day in a week because our Greek parents made us go, we did make the best of it. We just drove our Greek school teachers nuts, well at least I did. I wouldn't do my work when told to do so, I would throw paper balls across the room when the teacher wasn't looking, and I would just not pay any attention to anything. I always spoke in class with my friends while the teacher was teaching us and I would get into trouble. I had the loudest voice, so that's why I got caught first all the time. The teacher knew I was the instigator. My punishment was to write on the blackboard, about 25 times, "I will not speak in class", and I mastered how to spell this sentence in Greek. I was a pest, I knew it, but my Greek school teachers always had a soft spot for me because they loved my chubby little face. When it came time to do recitals for special Greek holidays where we did small plays and recited poems in Greek, I was the first one to want to participate because I loved being on stage. I guess my participation excused the fact that I was a pest. Well at least that is what I believed.

After Greek school was done we had Greek dancing from 1pm until 2pm. This is where we learned traditional Greek dances from all parts of Greece. This was my favorite part of the dreaded Saturday that I enjoyed most and my heart started to pound with delight when it was time to learn Greek dancing. I loved music, I loved to dance and I loved being on stage.

As I grew up I started to love Greek dancing more and more and Greek school wasn't so bad, I became fluent in Greek. Greek schools typically went up to grade eight and then we graduated from learning Greek and torturing our Greek school teachers. After the Greek school dance group, I later joined the senior Greek dance group of our Greek community and the ages ranged from 16 to people well into their 20s. Our teacher was Tom Zafiridis. In this group we learned more Greek dances and we would perform for various Hamilton events and also at our Greek community events. In my mid-20s the dance group dispersed, people went off to school, others got married and life's natural progression took over. I enjoyed being in the dance group very much, having lots of memories and making lifelong friends.

I still loved Greek dancing and didn't want to give it up. I heard from a friend a few years later tell me that the Greek community in London, Ontario was forming a dance group and this time people were from their 20s well into their 40s. I joined the group. I got in my car and drove about an hour and 15 minutes to get to London with other Hamilton friends that joined the group. I was excited because I could continue dancing. We practiced every Sunday for about two hours and there were about 30 people in the group. We also performed for various events too. Our dance teachers, a married couple, Tony and Paula Halkeas taught our group. We worked hard as a group. Well, okay, we socialized way too much at times, we argued and there was drama at times, but what do you expect when 30 Greek-Canadian people come together? In any case, we all worked hard, worked out our differences and here too we made lifelong friendships.

Now it was time to go to Greece with our dance group from London, Ontario. We worked hard for almost one year to put our 20 minute dance program together for it to be ready to perform in Greece. Our dance program included beautiful traditional costumes with every last detail done to perfection and we also sang at various points during our performance too. We also worked hard to fundraise 23 000 dollars in six months to help offset the cost of our trip. We hosted two Greek dances at a local club and went to just about every Greek business to get donations. In total, 26 dancers went to Greece. Each dancer only paid 840 dollars for 10 days which included flights, hotel and transportation.

We arrived the 10th of July in Athens where we spent the first five days of our trip. We were to perform at the Dora Stratou National Folk Theatre in Athens. There was a yearly dance festival for Greek dance groups of the diaspora to come and have a chance to perform at the theatre. The dates for this festival were from July 13th until the 16th. Greek dance groups came from Greek communities from all over the world. We were all looking forward to this amazing experience.

While in Athens our days were spent visiting sites like the Acropolis, the Agora and visiting the crystal blue beaches just outside of the city. Our evenings were spent going out for dinners, socializing and partying. I loved to party and I loved to socialize. I think I was the biggest party animal of the dance group and everybody knew I was up for a party at any time during the day or night. I had a great time visiting various bars and clubs in Athens. While having all this fun, we did fit in a dance practice or two before our scheduled performance.

We performed on the 15th in the evening. We arrived at the theatre, got dressed into our costumes with all kinds of emotions that filled the dressing room. Some were pacing back and forth, others were going over our songs, others were crying tears of joy, others were going over dance steps, others were trying to stay calm and not be nervous and the list went on and on. When we were finally ready and dressed, we left the dressing room and proceeded to the wings of the stage and waited our turn to perform. We waited in anticipation as the group before us was coming to an end. We were cued to get into position for our entrance dance. The music started to play and the lights started to fill the stage. We finally entered the stage. We danced our hearts out. The energy of the group was simply incredible. Our hands were held tightly with the person on either side of us. Our smiles were bright just like the sun's rays radiating on a hot summer's day. We danced to perfection; we were all on beat and not a single dancer made an error. It was the most amazing performance that we had ever done as a group. As we ended our show, the theatre was roaring with applause and we even got a standing ovation. We left overjoyed, hugging and kissing each other for the great work that we had just done. We left that evening to celebrate with food and drinks. The next day we left for the next five days of our trip, which was in the city of Rethymno on the island of Crete. It was one of the four major cities on the island. We performed in the main town square and there, too, the people enjoyed our performance. We spent our days and evenings just like we did in Athens, partying and having a good time.

SEPTEMBER 2007

I was now 27 years old, back from Greece and starting to search yet again for another dance studio to work at and I found one in Toronto. I still haven't found a professional dance partner and I don't have a steady dance job. So, I applied to this particular dance studio and I got the job. It was just the same as the other two studios that I worked for: businesses driven bosses, which was great and that's why they ran smoothly, but I was simply just handed manuals and DVDs that I still didn't understand how to use to teach myself and when I asked other dance colleagues for assistance they simply and politely said, "No."

They said no because they weren't paid to train and it wasn't their job. It was the owner's job. I was slowly discovering that I needed to work on my own to learn how to dance and stop relying on training from the studios. So, I started to make arrangements to do so and try to find a coach, yet I still didn't have a professional dance partner.

A girl I worked with suggested I sign up on a ballroom dance partner website because I was telling her how hard I was looking for one. In time, I found a young woman who lived in the greater Toronto area. Her name was Laura.

I was willing to work extremely hard to devote all my time and effort to practice, practice, practice like an Olympic athlete would train. Other professional ballroom dancers described that this was exactly what was needed to get done in order to succeed. I was willing! I was excited and we started practicing once a week. Well at this point I thought we would be retired and dead before we made it to the dance floor. So, I just said to myself, take what you can get and just shut it. Our personalities weren't compatible, but we did dance well together, so I thought I would give it a shot. We did a show at this fancy golf and country club at Christmas time. Laura walked into this club and demanded to speak with the organizer. I felt so embarrassed and I didn't say anything.

I didn't want to make the scene even worse than it already was. We were taken to a small boardroom to change and get ready for this show. Again, she was disappointed with the organizer because we had to share a room with the band that was playing for the event, yet the band was nice and let us change in their space. They were very accommodating even though she wasn't pleasant when she walked into the room and saw them.

Again, I felt embarrassed as she was changing. I left the room and apologized to the band and also to the organizer for her behaviour and luckily they said it was okay. I felt so much relief. I discovered after the show that we really weren't compatible. I said thank you for dancing with me and working with me. She smiled and we came to a mutual agreement by the end of December, 2007. So, I was on the quest to find a dance partner again.

I wondered what it would take to find a person who wanted to work hard, have fun at the same time and not argue with each other. In my mind, if there is no enjoyment in what you are doing, then what is the point of doing what you're doing? I was never afraid of hard work. I was always willing to get up at the crack of dawn to do whatever I needed to get the job done. In the dance world it's hard to maintain dance partner relationships because when you look for a dance partner the first thing you look for is dance compatibility and not personal compatibility, this is often why partnerships don't last because people only have dance in common.

JANUARY 2008

I was still working at the studio in Toronto, without any training whatsoever. I still didn't have a partner, yet I still held onto my dream of becoming a dancer, competitor, singer, actor and working for *Cirque du Soleil*. Oh, and let's not forget, I was still working at my family's Greek restaurant.

I was in no way, shape, or form ready to give up on my dream, not even close. Actually, I felt even more driven. I kept searching high and low for answers and clues about how to move forward. I talked to whomever I could to possibly move forward and pursue my crazy dream. I was advised to move to Toronto and quit commuting from Hamilton. I couldn't afford to live in Toronto. I wasn't making enough money and saving for coaching lessons. I kept hitting brick walls, yet I was just so determined. I just had to keep moving forward and I was saving my money to move forward in my career. I wasn't ready to move just yet.

In the meantime I was practicing hard with my students because at the end of the month, we had a pro-am competition. This time I was the "pro"; it was the first time I had ever danced in a competition with my students. They worked hard and were looking forward to the competition. I was excited to dance the entire day with my students. I had about 15 students that entered the competition. Each student had entered in about 10 to 20 heats for the day. I danced 240 heats, basically dancing non-stop the entire day. The competition was at the luxurious Royal York Hotel in downtown Toronto and the competition began at 9am. I started to dance, smile and just have a good time with each of my students on the dance floor. At about 11pm my boss approached me and said,

"Tasos you don't need to dance each dance with so much enthusiasm and energy, pace yourself, you're going to get tired".

I couldn't pace myself. I had to give each student my 110 percent of every fibre of my soul. It just wasn't an option to pace myself. They worked so hard to get to this point, having beautiful gowns that twinkled in the light and they were just full of excitement. I didn't want to let them down. I loved every minute dancing with them and I owed it to my students. It was important to me to deliver every last amount of energy that I had in my body. They trusted me to teach and dance with them and that's what I was going to give, period.

The dance competition ended at about 6pm and a formal dinner dance followed at about 7:30pm. This allowed for everybody to have a break and get ready for the dinner. I congratulated my students and left the dance floor. I was in so much foot pain that it was so unbearable, it felt like a car had run over my feet. Also, I was dripping sweat because I had danced so hard the entire day. I had to sit down for a while. I found an attendant that worked at the hotel and asked for a bucket of ice. I followed the attendant to the kitchen and got the ice, I then took my bucket and went to the farthest point to the other side of this huge hotel and away from the ballroom where nobody could see me, found a chair and put my feet in the ice for about 25 minutes. It felt amazing. My throbbing foot pain was leaving and my feet started to freeze from the ice and I truly felt relief. It was worth the pain and sweat. I owed it to my students, they trusted me as an instructor and in return I did my very best for them and I did. After my break I had a shower, put my tuxedo on and enjoyed a night of dinner and dancing.

MAKING SOME CHANGES

MAY 2008

I was 28 years old and discovered that the franchise dance business wasn't for me. I left for good. Even though it didn't work out at the previous three studios, I did like the franchise business because they had a good system of business in place. I just wished the studio owners would follow the code of conduct to train their staff.

I was working at a dance studio in Toronto with a girl by the name of Gina; she had a friend who competed. She owned a ballroom dance business, "Come Dancing" and her name was Karen. Gina introduced me to her. She was very nice and outgoing. She left the franchise dance world to start her own business and informed me that there was a world outside of the franchise dance world. This made me feel much better about my decision.

I was petrified to leave it and didn't know what to do at this point. Karen assured me that there is bigger and better dancing outside of the franchise world of dance, with plenty of coaches that would help me, teach me and help me understand the crazy dance manuals. I was so excited and I asked her if she wanted to dance with me professionally, well, I practically begged and she said she was done with competing. I was disappointed that she didn't want to dance and I respected her decision and we became very good friends. Karen coached me and I started training with her for free, and I appreciated her kindness. She helped me to understand dancing, and the manuals, which was very helpful. I felt much happier. I was finally getting somewhere.

A TASTE OF ARCHAEOLOGY

JULY 2008

I travelled to Greece on an archaeological excavation and had a fantastic time. I was on the island of Antikythera, a tiny little island below the Peloponnese. The population, at that time, was about 65 people. The island is about 20 square kilometers if I am not mistaken. It was full of valleys, mountains and pebbled beaches with breath taking views. I had been excavating on the island for a few summers beforehand and I loved it. For the most part people on the island enjoyed our company; however, there were others that didn't. They didn't like the fact that people had come to this quiet little island and disrupted their lives.

There were only a few who were discontented, though they could be vocal about it at times. One morning, an islander started yelling at the head archaeologist. He told him to stop digging up the island and go home. In any case, it was so nice to be there, breathing fresh Mediterranean air and having good food in the evenings in the only tavern on the island. We had a good time with most of the local people. We drank with them and told them how our excavations were going on a day-to-day basis. Most of the islanders felt a part of the excavation because we were updating them on what was happening.

And here is a side note, it has no relevance whatsoever to the excavation, but aside from having a doctor on the island, there also was a police station. It was in the main port along with the tavern.

The police station had a single cell and an office and because of the non-existent crime on the island, I wondered why on earth they needed a police station here. One afternoon I went to the tavern and had an ice-cream and saw the police officer there. He was never dressed in his uniform, but I guess he didn't need to be.

I sat down and asked him, "What kind of crime could there possibly be here on this island?"

He started laughing, "There's nothing at all, just people complaining about chickens going missing."

I laughed with him, finished my ice-cream and walked up the hill to our residence where we were staying with the other archaeologists. It was hotter than Hades and in the middle of the afternoon, a 20-minute walk in the heat felt like an hour.

Our residence was a campsite we had made in the old school yard that nobody used anymore. The one-room schoolhouse was made into the lab where we bagged artefacts and wrote our daily journals of what happened on site. We had about 15 tents in the schoolyard (that we had put up) and in total we were about 20 archaeologists, most of them were first year students.

We got up every morning at 6am and started our 30-minute walk down the hill to the port only to go up hill again to our site. At the main beach, where I wasn't digging, was the foundation of the Temple of Apollo. It was his temple because about 100 years ago his statue was found on that very spot. I had the luxury of going uphill to dig in a cave. The cave had some niches inside and we were trying to see what its use was. Some believe ceremonial because of the niches inside of it; anyway, it was out of the hot sun. Working on excavations was fun and I enjoyed them, even if they were hard work.

Excavating was done by noon and then we had lunch. It was the only time we could have a shower because there was one public shower in the one public washroom and 20 people needed to bathe daily, so you can only imagine how much time we had to shower — not very much. There was no running water at the school. When you're digging for history it's not glamorous. Sometimes you don't find anything for weeks and you have all this amazing historical rubble that you have to piece together, with lots of missing pieces to the puzzle, trying to make sense of the evidence.

LOTS OF DANCING

OCTOBER 2008

I was teaching with my new friend Karen, I still didn't have a dance partner, but I enjoyed my new job. I never cancelled my subscription to the ballroom dance partner website and I would look on my profile from time to time to see if I had any dance partner requests. I put on my profile that I was willing to relocate because that is how badly I wanted to dance.

One day I got a message from a girl in Philadelphia who was interested in meeting. Her name was Susan. I declined. Even though I was willing to do whatever it took to make my dream come true, I was too afraid to leave my home and go that far away.

Well, I read this message on a Monday and on Friday I messaged Susan to meet because I was tossing and turning in my sleep all week. I could have been throwing my dream away. It was always on my mind during the day, in the evening and in my dreams. So, I emailed Susan to meet and she agreed.

I was really excited. I know I am always getting excited and it doesn't take much sometimes. I asked my new friend and boss Karen to come to Philly with me. It would be an eight-hour journey by car. It was such a beautiful drive; the leaves were at their best this time of the year. The red, gold, yellow and orange leaves were ready to fall.

We arrived at the hotel in the early evening. Susan paid for the room. We were scheduled for a tryout the next morning. It was at 11am and I was excited. We had our dance tryout and I felt it went great in my mind. I was so excited and I just wanted to dance; though she was a fantastic dancer I was just not good enough for her. As a result, she wasn't interested in dancing with me. I was disappointed, I said thank you and left that afternoon to go back home.

I was glad I went because I found out the facts. It didn't work out, but I attained peace of mind and received an answer.

NOVEMBER 2008

I was still working at my same dance job and loving it: still no dance partner, but I wasn't giving up. I looked again on the ballroom partner website and saw I had a message from a girl in Toronto. Her name was Judy. We agreed to dance together and met with her coach Tanya Cardinal.

I had saved money to start taking lessons, so I was ready. Tanya was amazing and I really clicked with this woman. I met with my new coach once a week and she was helping me with all the material and I slowly started to understand the material in the dance manuals. I was super happy.

I was so excited to be dancing at a much higher level and finally making sense of these dance manuals. Judy and I met at least three times a week at her apartment and danced in her living room. It was big enough to practice, rather than renting studio space. Then, she started cancelling and I was getting upset. I said if we are serious about this we must work hard. It seemed like she wasn't into dancing as much as I was, so we slowly started disagreeing and it lead to us arguing about everything. Well, this new dance partner relationship wasn't working out and we weren't getting along. We came to a mutual agreement and called it quits at about February 2009, but I did start using her dance coach Tanya. She was fantastic and later on Judy left the dance business altogether. The benefit of meeting her was that she introduced me to my new amazing coach. As I see it, good things come out of any situations that don't work out.

FEBRUARY 2009

I was still enjoying my dance job with my friend and boss, Karen. Plus, I had a fantastic group of students, but it wasn't busy enough for me to work full-time. I was working on a part-time basis from the beginning.

Then, a couple that I was teaching, Connie and Carm, told me they came across an advertisement that a dance studio in Woodbridge was hiring dance teachers. I said I was interested and on their next lesson with me they brought me the information. I called "Ciao Bella Dance Studio" and spoke with the owner. Her name was Dana and she told me the position was just filled. I was disappointed, but she did say she would keep me in mind if she needed instructors in the future. Normally, in the dance business, when a studio owner says they are going to keep your information they keep it, I was hoping she would.

From my experience, the problem in the dance world is that dance teachers are hard to find, especially male dance teachers. There are just not enough of them, there are more single women that want to take up dancing as a sport or hobby than there are men. That's just how it goes.

MAY 2009

I got a phone call at the beginning of May. It was Dana and she asked me to come in for an interview because there was a position available. I said yes and was very excited. I walked into the dance studio and was greeted by Dana, a short, curvy, and vivacious, woman in her late 40s who loved to swear and was very animated. She immediately called me *Tasos Cazzos* (*cazzo* means penis in Italian and it rhymed with my name) which turned into "Tasos catsos". I know — hilarious. This is how this nickname came to be. I didn't mind, it was funny. I sat down with her and had an interview. She loved me and gave me a job. She was making jokes and laughing the whole time.

Dana was such a different person. I loved her style instantly. I had never worked with a boss like her in my life. It was a different kind of atmosphere, but it worked for her and it did for me too. I wanted to be in a pleasant work environment and this was more than pleasant. It was fun!

I maintained my job at the other dance studio with Karen. I still didn't have a dance partner, but I had my profile on the ballroom partner website. I started teaching two beginner classes at the studio on Monday nights and two intermediate classes on Tuesday nights. I really enjoyed working there. They let me enjoy teaching and the love I had for dance. Plus, I could still work at my family's burger joint.

I had a good time with the students. I could be myself, not a salesman selling dance lessons. I didn't have to deal with the sales at all. The owner dealt with the sales and I was there to strictly teach, which made me happy and more at ease. It was the right fit for me.

OCTOBER 2009

In October I got a message on my profile from a girl in New Hampshire. Her name was Grace. I emailed Grace telling her how serious I was about my dancing career and that I wanted to take it as far as possible. We agreed to meet. I got in my car and drove nine hours to meet her and have a dance tryout.

This time I drove alone and sang to whatever song came through the radio. I arrived in the evening and we met the next morning. She played a waltz, a tango and a foxtrot; then we took a break and started to chat and get to know each other. Then we danced a cha cha, a rumba and ended with a bolero. I felt it went well. It was the most dancing I had ever done at a dance partner tryout and I was very excited. I knew Grace was married and I asked her if her husband was okay with us dancing together. She said they had spoken about it and there was nothing to worry about.

I suggested to come down for a week once a month to practice and she agreed. We made a plan that in four months we would start competing and we would work like crazy every time I came down to practice. We agreed to enter into the American Rhythm division. I left the next day thinking we would be dance partners. I got home and after my nine-hour drive with plans to go down again in a few weeks.

The next few weeks went by, it was now the end of October and I was ready to drive back down to New Hampshire. The studios I worked for were willing to accommodate my schedule. They said a studio looks good when their instructors are competitors. They believe it's more enticing for people to dance. When it was time for me to leave I checked my email. This is what she wrote ...

Oh I have had a terrible accident and broke my foot unfortunately I can't dance with you and I will email you when I get better.

I was so disappointed that she didn't have the common courtesy to call and tell me. It was only by chance that I checked my email before I was going to leave. I could have driven all the way to New Hampshire for nothing. I would have been really angry if I got there and didn't know about this important piece of information.

I think she just wasn't interested in dancing with me and she didn't have the common courtesy to tell me. I went to sleep that night and proceeded with my next day as usual. Here is a good point of advice that I learned from this situation: always check your emails, Facebook, texts etc., before departing for a meeting just in case something goes wrong or is cancelled. Never assume, like I did. Confirm your plans before you go.

NOVEMBER 2009

I was still working at both jobs, at Ciao Bella Dance Studio in Woodbridge and with Karen too. I was very happy and my crazy fun boss Dana created a comfortable atmosphere and I loved teaching there. I was teaching regularly and had plenty of students and still managed to help my parents out at our family restaurant too.

I was still training with my dance coach Tanya Cardinal and she was helping me prepare for my dance exams. I checked my messages on my ballroom dance profile and saw a message from another girl in Toronto. Her name was Lauren.

She lived and taught at a studio in the south end of Toronto. We met at her studio one evening to get to know each other and share our dancing goals. I got my dancing coach Tanya to choreograph the swing and cha cha routines and used my own creativity to choreograph the rumba, bolero and mambo routines.

We were preparing to compete in the American Rhythm Section in the professional division. We practiced three to four times a week for about two to three hours every time. I would wake up at 6am and drive in to Toronto from Hamilton to beat the traffic. I had to be in the city before 9am.

I would arrive early to Lauren's studio and she would always be late. She lived five minutes away from the studio. I never said anything and kept a zipper on my mouth because I really wanted to dance. We learned all five routines and did a small show in Toronto. I was happy with the performance. It was my first paid show in a very, very long time.

I was working hard doing competitive routines with her and she would yell at me and argue with me every time I made a mistake, but when she was making errors I was patient and nice to her. We also flew to Montreal to see a choreographer where he added additional moves to our routines and helped us clean them up.

Finally, at the beginning of February 2010 I had enough of this dance partner relationship and her attitude. I blew up at her and called it quits. We were supposed to be dancing because we were enjoying it and it became very labour intensive. I wasn't having fun; there was no pleasure to dance anymore. I walked out and never spoke to her again. A few months later I was checking my emails and she sent me a message. She apologized for her bad behaviour and stated that she was going through a rough time in her life and didn't mean to do it. I replied and said that's fine and that it was okay.

I learned not to allow situations to get out of hand. If I find something is bothering me, I must speak rather than not say anything at all. I don't say anything to avoid arguing, because I wanted to dance, but I let it fester inside of me and then I blew up, it wasn't good. Communication is key to any relationship, talking through problems and situations will allow for a better working environment and not lead to blowing up and leaving. I'll make a note of that for next time and speak nicely rather than blowing up.

MARCH 2010

At this time I decided to take my first dance exam. I did it through the Canadian Dancesport Federation. I had some good training basics from my coach Tanya, yet I needed more. I was still struggling to make ends meet and was spending all of my money to get training in all my fields. I thought I was ready for the exam, so instead of using my coach as a dance partner I danced with my friend Karen. She is a fantastic dancer. I just couldn't afford to pay for my coach to dance with me for my exam.

For my first exam the examiner's name was Alan Armsby. It was the American Rhythm exam. The dances I had to dance were the cha cha, rumba, mambo, bolero, East Coast swing, West Coast swing, samba and merengue. I had to dance all of the dances in a routine as a male and then as a female. I was the dance leader and then we did a role reversal where she was the dance leader and I was the follower. As an instructor you have to know both genders in order to teach them.

After that I was questioned on all eight dances. The dancing was the easy part. The questions on theory were the hard part. It was 15 steps per dance (I had to also know the female steps too, so it was about 30 steps per dance in the end for each dance) and I was asked questions about foot work, foot positions, amount of turn, and could be asked any questions on either male or female dance steps.

The examiner Alan was fair and kind. I wasn't prepared enough. I started to sweat when asked detailed questions about the steps. I was nervous and uncomfortable and my heart was pounding. I was wiping my sweat on my sleeve because I was sweating so much and finally the examiner told me to go to the washroom and wipe my face.

I was praying deep down inside that I would do well. I knew I needed more training and I didn't have enough money so I just struggled through the studying having many questions and nobody to ask, but I passed the exam.

I felt a sigh of relief and it was as though a ton of bricks had been lifted off of my shoulders. I felt I was in school again doing end of term exams, boy, I didn't miss that. The difference here was with these exams they are all oral, you can't write anything on paper and hope to get part marks. It was all or nothing during these intense examinations. It was hard because of my lack of coaching, but I made it and attained my Level One Teaching Certificate in American Rhythm. I left the studio, called some friends and texted other friends. They were all happy for me.

MAY 2010

I was still working in Woodbridge at Ciao Bella Dance Studio for my funny boss Dana and I was still working for my friend Karen in her business from time to time. I finally met a new dance partner through a Brazilian samba team that I had been dancing with for the past few months. She was a trained bachata, merengue and salsa dancer. Her name was Mary. I asked her if she wanted to learn how to dance my dance style and compete professionally because I was having no luck with dance partners. She agreed. I started teaching Mary to dance my level of style and technique. We met four days a week and practiced about two to three hours a day. I trained her and I choreographed our routines. She was receptive and willing to learn so we could dance.

We entered in both the American Rhythm and American Smooth categories. It was a crazy amount of work, but with her work ethic and mine I knew we could pull it off. We trained hard, didn't argue and it was nice to work with somebody that I got along with. We worked well together and hard too. We just clicked; it was fantastic.

JULY 2010

All was going well at this point, I was working at the studio, had a new dance partner, having great students, still training with my coach Tanya, working at my parents' restaurant on the weekends, and studying to make more sense of these dance manuals to prepare for my next dance exam.

I wasn't seeing my dance coach as often as I would have liked. It was too expensive and I was saving as much as money as I could for dance coaching. For my next dance exam I was going to dance it with an advanced student of mine, Connie, who danced very well. I was learning more and more of this dance syllabus, but trying to verbalize dance steps and being very technical was the nightmare. Even though I didn't feel ready for the exam because I still needed more help, I went ahead and booked my exam anyway. I got my student Connie to dance the routines with me.

The time was slowly approaching and I was feeling the same way I felt during my last exam: extremely nervous. The exam was scheduled for the end of July with the same nice examiner, Alan Armsby. I did my dance demonstration, dancing the routines and they went well. I dreaded the next part where the examiner started asking questions about the dance steps.

The examiner began asking me questions on the theory part of the exam. I couldn't answer the questions. I stopped the exam and asked the examiner if I could do it another time. I felt so unprepared and nervous because deep down inside I knew I wasn't ready for this dance exam. I realized I needed more training and somebody to help me understand the dance manuals.

Alan, the examiner, understood my struggles both financially and in understanding the material. He advised me to keep practicing and it would all come together at some point and, "When you're ready come back and do the exam again."

I agreed. I was well on my way to understanding them, I just needed more time and training. I called Tanya and asked for more lessons. I decided to start seeing her for three, 45 minute sessions every Tuesday at $75 dollars a session. It was going to cost me $225. It was my dream to be a dancer and it just needed to get done, period. I was spending about $900 a month on my dance coach, which was a big chunk of my income. She was trained in the International styles and she knew how to read and understand the dance manuals, which I was studying. There are two styles of ballroom dancing: International and American. She knew and understood the methods of reading the manuals and she was teaching me how to understand them the way she did. She was fantastic and extremely knowledgeable.

The International styles have two divisions. The Latin division with the cha cha, rumba, jive, paso doble and samba and the Standard with the foxtrot, waltz, tango, Viennese waltz and quick-step. The American divisions were developed out of the International divisions. They were created so people could learn how to dance the International styles in social settings; modifications to the dances had been made making it easier for people to learn. This style is taught in most social studios.

There are two divisions in the American styles as well. The American Rhythm with the cha cha, rumba, swing, mambo and bolero, and the American Smooth with the waltz, foxtrot, tango and Viennese waltz. At that time the American styles had become just as popular in all dance competitions and had a professional division to them too. I started learning the American styles and I choose to compete in the American Smooth and Rhythm professional divisions. All four styles were amazing, having their beauty and flare to each dance.

SEPTEMBER 2010

The summer had come and gone and all was going well for me.

I registered for singing lessons at the Hamilton Conservatory for the Arts, under the direction of Roland Fix. The last time I sang and danced was just after university when I did some community theatre. I was adding more to my already busy schedule, but I loved it.

I had lessons every Thursday evening at 7pm for 45 minutes. I was just plain busy. This was a typical work week for me: Monday morning I practiced with my dance partner Mary and in the evening I would teach dancing; Tuesday I met with my dance coach Tanya so we could continue working on my dance material and I taught in the evening; Wednesday I taught students in the morning at a local school, dance practice in the afternoon with my dance partner and taught in the evening; Thursday I had dance practice all day and singing lessons in the evening; Friday I had dance practice during the day and worked at the family restaurant; Saturday I was working at the family restaurant in the evening; and Sunday I taught all day. It was fantastic. I always knew being versatile was good and it was necessary to be able to sing, dance and act on stage — and that's what I was trying to do.

NOVEMBER 2010

The next few months went according to my plan. My dance partner Mary and I performed in our first show, it was for the *Food and Wine Show* at the Toronto Convention Centre. It was a huge convention with booths of exotic foods and wine from all over the world and local products too.

We made our way to the event coordinator and he gave us tickets to enter the show, giving us the opportunity to taste different wines and foods. It was delicious. Afterwards we were directed to the dance area. We danced on a carpeted area in the lobby where we could barely hear the music in the background. It was a dancer's nightmare. People were talking and we couldn't hear the music because they had only one small speaker, the type that you would have in your home. It was a huge lobby so it didn't work well and to top it all off, we had to dance on carpet, which made it harder to move gracefully. We danced a foxtrot and a tango; though, with all of these difficulties we made it look fantastic. We were now professionals and we handled it well. She wore a pink and white ball gown and I wore a black vest and a sparkly tie.

DECEMBER 2010

Everything was still going great and I couldn't be any happier. After practicing three hours a week with my dance coach Tanya on my dance material, I was finally ready to take my dance exam. It was scheduled for December 16th, 2010. I worked hard and finally had a good grasp and understanding of the dance manuals. I was ready to do my first level exam in my American Smooth dancing.

I went to the studio and had the same dance examiner, Alan Armsby. I received a 75 percent on my overall testing. I did extremely well on the dance demonstration with my coach and on the verbal part I did well too. I was so happy because I finally understood how to read and use the manuals properly. Also, the week before my dance exam I had my first singing recital. I got up on stage wearing black dress pants and a shirt. I was the last one to sing in my group. The ages ranged from young children to older seniors. They loved the art of singing. I sang **Mr. Cellophane** from the musical **Chicago**. I was so excited and jumping for joy inside. As I was leaving the recital hall my music coach Roland Fix complimented me and so did many people watching the show. It was such a nice feeling to hear all these compliments, I was so happy.

After that, I took off for a month and went to visit family and friends in Greece. While there, I went to see a judge from Dancing **with the Stars** in Greece. I wanted to get on the show in Greece and the best way was trying to find one of the judges, so I did.

Her name was Galena and she owned three dance studios in Athens. I called and asked if she was available for me to meet her. She agreed so I went to her studio and spoke with her for about an hour. We spoke about life and of course dancing, and I expressed how much I wanted to be on **Dancing with the Stars** in Greece. She was pleasant, warm and very inviting. I was happy with our conversation and I said I would like to stay in touch with her and she agreed. I told her that I was going to come back again to do whatever it takes to get on to the show. She smiled and I left the studio. I was pleased with our meeting.

COMPETITIONS

JANUARY 2011

I continued working with my dancing coach Tanya and I was over the moon happy because I had a great meeting in Greece and had completed both of my first levels in the American dancing divisions.

I started working on my International Standard exams with my coach and was excited to be learning both the American and International styles because generally dancers only choose one or the other. There was a colossal amount of work involved and I was willing to do it. I would be one of the few teachers in Canada certified in both styles. I was ready for the challenge.

My dance partner Mary and I were ready for our first competition in Niagara Falls. We entered in both divisions of the American styles, Smooth and Rhythm. We worked hard and were ready to dance. We placed last in both divisions, but we were happy because it was our first event.

As we were leaving, we went to get our results at the information table by the entrance. We were greeted by a nice lady and she complimented us on our dancing. We graciously said thank you.

Then out of the blue she looked at us and said,

"You know you both dance beautifully, but it will be a long time before you get even close to winning, you have to wait your turn."

I knew what she meant. There is plenty of politics in the ballroom world, just like anything else. I didn't want to believe what I just heard, but I knew it for a truth. My dance partner looked at me with a puzzled look on her face. I brought her into this dance world and slowly I was letting her know about the "ballroom games" you had to play, but I hadn't explained this to her yet.

I said, "I will explain later." I did explain later what happened and she was just as disgusted as I was. Talent is only a part in winning, seeing the judges before a competition was the key to winning too. In other words, when you enter a competition you need to find out who the judges are beforehand. You hire a judge that costs anywhere from $75 to $145 to get a 45-minute coaching session so they "know" who you are on the dance floor and would mark you better. Get the politics now?

MARCH 2011

My dance partner Mary and I entered into our second competition in Dearborn, Michigan. We drove just over four hours to compete. It was a smaller competition and we were finalists in both the American Rhythm and Smooth divisions, which made us very happy and proud of ourselves. We got $1000 dollars, which just covered all of our expenses (hotel and entry fee) for the three days. Gas, food and any other incidentals came out of our own pockets.

After that, between having a break and some free time on my hands, I was wondering how I was going to get to Greece again to hand in my resume for *Dancing with the Stars*. I believed I would have to fly there again, but only for a short period of time.

I sat myself in front of the computer and booked a ticket to Greece for five days at the end of June on my credit card. God bless credit cards and the inventor of them, I just booked it on my card, screamed for joy in front of the computer like an animal and wondered how I was going to pay for this brief but quick trip.

I was nervous because I hadn't even called the production company and I had a ticket. I figured if I wanted to be on the show, I had to show people in Greece that I was serious and going in person would be the best way.

APRIL 2011

My dance partner Mary and I continued practicing hard and as often as we could. I entered us in a dance competition in Philadelphia. The dance floor was full of dancers, as usual, with women in beautiful gowns and men in tuxedos in the Smooth and Standard divisions. The Rhythm and Latin divisions were aligned with dancers with sexy women in hot dresses and the guys wore fitted shirts and pants.

We placed as finalists again in both divisions and got about $1000 dollars, which once again covered all our competition expenses. Gas, food and other incidentals came out of our pockets. At this point, I was still taking coaching lessons with my coach and learning the International style Latin division manuals. I was ready to take the first level of the Latin division exam. I took it again with the same examiner, Alan Armsby, and I got 75 percent. I was still nervous during the exam, but I felt a little less nervous than usual, which was fantastic. I was happy with the results and after the test I started studying for the International Standard division.

MAY 2011

This time I entered us into a competition in Atlantic City. It was almost a ten-hour drive to the next best gambling place to Vegas. We drove through endless highways of trees, hills and mountains. Finally, as we were approaching the city at night, we saw a bright strip of lights as if it were the sun setting in the distance — but it wasn't. It was the main strip of casinos and hotels lighting up the night sky. We checked into the hotel and got up early in the morning to go over our dance routines before the main ballroom opened for the competition. We then took the rest of the day to explore Atlantic City. It was a nice sunny day. The city is on the coast of the Atlantic Ocean. It has white sandy beaches and a boardwalk lined with casinos, but it wasn't warm enough to go swimming. We walked in and out of the casinos, shops and then just took a walk on the sand until the early evening. We had dinner and practiced before we went on the dance floor late in the evening. We entered in the same divisions and were finalists once again winning about $1000 dollars, which again covered our same expenses.

JUNE 2011

My trip to Greece was slowly approaching. Well, it was at the end of the month, but before my trip we had a competition in Chicago and I still hadn't contacted the people who were in charge of the *Dancing with the Stars* in Greece.

We drove nine hours and to cut costs we stayed with relatives of mine. This was one of the bigger competitions in the United States and there must have been about 50 couples per division. We didn't place as finalists, we didn't come close, but we weren't last. I was fine with that just as long as we didn't come last. We didn't win any money and so we had to cover all of our costs. It was nice that my cousins and aunt came to see our competition and I got to spend time with family, which was great. It's always nice to have fans in the audience. We also did some sightseeing and made a nice trip out of it.

We came home and got back to practicing again as usual. Around the second week of June I heard about a Greek Orthodox priest who had show business connections in Greece. I called him and told him my story and asked if there was any way he could help me to speak with anybody in Greece. He told me to email him my resume and I did. I appreciated his help, but I never heard from him again. I didn't follow up with him either and he seemed like he was busy, so I was just going to have to call Greece myself.

On June 23rd, I stayed up until 5am to book appointments in Greece. I also called Judge Fokkas, who was on *Dancing with the Stars*. I wanted to see if he could give me some advice, but his manager said he was busy. He was the official host for the Special Olympics in Greece at that time and very busy.

Then I called Ant1, the main television network in Greece and they put me through to the ENA Productions, the production company working with them. I spoke with the producer and told him I was coming from Canada to hand in my resume in person. We set up the appointment and I left that Sunday. I told a bunch of my friends and cousins that I was going. They all thought I was a nut, but admired my perseverance and drive and were very supportive.

MY SHORT TRIP TO GREECE

JUNE 29, 2011

I was sitting on my close friend Dora's veranda in a suburb of Athens. I'm staying with her and her family in Athens. From their home I can look down at the city and see the Acropolis and Lykavittos Hill. It's a cloudy, yet warm day and today there are protests going on in Syntagma Square out front of the parliament buildings. The protest is in concern of the debt crisis in Greece. All the protests are happening in front of the parliament buildings. The protesters didn't want to hurt any civilians, and they never did, even though the media would sometimes make it look like it. They just wanted to be heard and nothing else. The rest of Athens is calm and people are carrying on with their daily routine as usual while waiting in anticipation of what the outcome will be. The sound of birds, cars and voices keep me company as I write.

I had called Judge Fokkas and the casting director from ENA Productions from the airport when I first landed. The casting director was pleasant and I made an appointment with him for the following day between noon and 1pm. I couldn't get a hold of Fokkas. His manager told me to email my resume and my contact information, I told her I was going to drop off a resume package at the studio. Again, she told me that it was going to be hard to speak with him because he was hosting the Special Olympics in Athens.

At Dora's I told her my five-day plan and her father helped me to write a formal letter in Greek. It was amazing and so well written. He was a successful lawyer and had a great way of speaking and writing.

Her father left the room and I started to laugh. She asked, "Why are you laughing?"

I responded, "You know, I can speak, read, and write Greek well, but this is over the top. Whoever reads this will know I didn't write it."

We laughed and sent this very professional Greek letter out anyway. Dora suggested that I find the production company where my appointment was to be the next day. I agreed, so we got into my rental car and went on our merry way. We had an address, but no map, though we knew the general area where ENA Productions was located.

After two hours of searching the area and asking people how to find the street, we finally found the place. I realized that next time I should bring a map or a GPS: lesson learned.

Dora said, "Aren't you glad we found it today? You never would have found it during the morning rush hour." I agreed.

After that we went to the centre of Athens to Kypseli Avenue where Judge Fokkas' dance studio was located. Dora knew where this street was and I was familiar with the area too. We parked the car and I took my resume package (headshots, reference letters, copies of my resume in Greek and English and a DVD of me dancing) to find the studio. We buzzed and were let in by a nice, pleasant, blonde woman who took my information and put it on Fokkas' desk.

By then it was about 10:45pm and we were both hungry. I started naming some cool areas in Athens to eat, like Gazi and Exarchia. Exarchia is more of a punk, metal and alternative crowd and Gazi is more mainstream. We went to Gazi, walked around and finally sat down at a restaurant just off the main drag with loud music and people walking in and out of the clubs and restaurants.

We ate, drank and caught up with each other's lives while laughing and having some serious, deep conversations too. All of a sudden we saw the nice blonde woman from the studio. I point her out and Dora and I look at each other in awe. In a city of about five million people, and of all places, we see her an hour later. Wow! We took it as a positive sign. Finally, we leave and call it a day because I was tired from the long flight and an eventful day.

Now it's June 28th and the very day I was going to ENA Productions. I got up at 8am because I was told the night before that there may be a transportation strike and it may take a long time to get to the production company, which was only a 30-minute drive. So, I enjoyed breakfast with Dora's mom and left the house at 9:45am. I got there at about 10:30am, parked my rental car and walked around the two malls located in the area to kill some time.

At 11:30am I drove down the street to the production company. I walked into the building and was greeted by the receptionist rolling her cigarette at her desk. This is Greece; it's a nice, pleasant and relaxed country. I asked where the director's office was, she gave me directions and I found his office.

The pleasant director greeted me and started off with some small talk and then called in his assistant to conduct a full casting. I was a lucky guy. They wouldn't do this for anybody because it was not the casting date for the show. I think it was because of my determination and that I came from half way across the world just to meet them in person.

His assistant took me into the studio and asked me if I had any TV experience, I said no. I went into a lengthy description of my dancing career and told them I sang too, did shows and that I was a professional ballroom and Latin dance competitor. That was the dry run through to make me feel comfortable in front of the camera.

She then turned on the camera and lights and started to ask me questions about my life and myself and if I can handle working with a celebrity because they can be difficult and I said, yes I can handle anything. I then proceeded to tell her I have been teaching people of all ages my whole career. She also asked me how do I handle problematic situations? I said with a smile and never get stressed out because with stress nothing gets done. Then we went into a description about myself, my travels around the world, hobbies and other interests too. She seemed impressed.

Then I showed her my colourful resume package. She responded with a smile and said, "Wow, we always look for this kind of stuff and never get it, well done." She said it wasn't necessary to come in January and February for the auditions because they had my information. I was extremely happy of how the meeting panned out.

I spent that evening at Dora's house with her cousin Dimitri and his friend. At midnight our friend Oresti came over for a few drinks and we stayed up until 4:30am eating ice-cream and looking at my dance videos. He showed us his archaeological photos and I said I would come and take some more for him because I have a certificate in art photography with a specialization in archaeological photography along with my degree in Classics and a certificate in world archaeology.

Today is June 29th, and I got up at 4pm because I was still jetlagged and I was exhausted. Dora was teaching at her music academy and I was writing my journal when she came home around 7pm. We ate and watched the news to see the havoc that was going on in Syntagma Square with all the protests and then went to visit our friend Averkio. At his place we ate, chatted with his sister and parents and stayed until 3am talking about the financial crisis in Greece.

MY JOURNEY TO MY DREAM

JUNE 30, 2011

I set my alarm for 9am. I shut it off and kept sleeping. I was now leaving to go back home to Canada. Dora's mom knocked on my door at 10:10am to remind me of the time because she knew I had a flight to catch. It was a 30-minute drive to the airport, it was nearby, but I still was cutting it close.

I showered, got dressed, had something to eat, said goodbye, went to the airport, returned my car and checked in. My flight was scheduled for 2:35pm, it was delayed because the flight left Brussels late. The flight was nice with just a little turbulence. We arrived in Brussels at 5pm and I quickly made my way to the information desk and asked where the best place to go to in the city.

The pleasant woman suggested that I go and visit the most beautiful city centre (in her opinion) in all of Europe. She gave me a map and I was on my way. I put my bags in a locker, took some cash and my identification, and went on my merry way into the city.

I arrived at the city centre greeted by buildings built in the late 1600s into the 1700s. I was stunned with amazement at how beautiful the square looked. I had never seen anything so beautiful in my life and I had visited about 20 countries up to this point in my life.

It was like a dream, a fairy tale filled with ornate buildings with carvings and with statues decorating each building. I stood in awe taking it all in. I took so many photos, but pictures don't do it justice because of how spectacular the place really was. The lady at the information desk at the airport was right. It is one of the most beautiful squares I have ever seen in Europe.

I spent the afternoon walking up and down the streets stuffing my face with chocolate and I even had a true Belgian waffle too. How could you be in Belgium and not have these fantastic treats? I couldn't resist. I caught the 11:03pm train back to the airport and found a place to sleep on the floor. I had a 10:30am flight the next morning.

From my experience, this is the life of an artist; not being able to afford a hotel room and spending your money on trying to fulfill your dreams. If you can get past the humps, bumps and blocks of your starvation period you will find nothing but success at the end of your tunnel. I truly believe it. I didn't know how long it would take, but I knew it would happen at some point. If I don't believe it, then who will? Ah, so big deal, I sleep in the airport. It's not the first time and at this point it won't be the last time either, it just adds to my adventure. Tomorrow I leave for home.

CIRQUE DU SOLEIL

JULY 2011

Now I was back home and my dance partner Mary and I are practicing for our next competition which will be held at the beginning of the month in Montreal. We had free time during the day because we were competing at 11:30pm — yes, that's right, at night.

All the competitions we enter are about three days in length and the professional divisions are usually the last to compete, starting with the junior divisions to the amateur divisions. It was about 10am on the day of our competition and we had the whole day to ourselves. Mary had work to do and I just spent the day alone with a plan in mind.

As I have mentioned, I had a big dream of singing, dancing and acting with *Cirque du Soleil*. I walked out of the hotel and headed for the subway station that would take me to their headquarters in Montreal. I got off at the Jean Talon Station and I walked to their office. As I was approaching the building I could see this massive structure in the distance. It was big, beautiful and colourful, just like the circus.

I went in and asked to speak with the person in charge of singing, dancing and acting. I waited for a few minutes and this nice young lady (maybe a few years older than me) with brown hair and brown eyes introduced herself with a warm smile and shook my hand, her name was Mary Claude Vincent. I told her I wanted to work for *Cirque du Soleil*.

She asked, "Have you been on our website?"

I said, "Yes, I could practically act it out!" I told her I knew it inside out. She smiled and laughed and so did I. I told her I wanted to know some information that wasn't available on their website. I wanted to know more about the circus and that I wanted to work there because I loved every aspect of it, from travelling to performing and meeting new people.

I knew that was for me. It was the perfect fit. She went on and told me information from the history of *Cirque du Soleil* to the working environment and everything in between. It lasted about 45 minutes. She said the best thing to do is send a DVD with all of my talent. I said that I would put something together and bring it down, she said it wasn't necessary, just up load it on the website.

I said I wanted to bring it down to prove I was really interested because I knew I wasn't the only one on the planet that wanted to work for this fantastic company. I left happy and thankful that somebody gave me their time.

It was late afternoon when I got back to the hotel. I had a nap, got up in the early evening to practice with my dance partner and was ready to compete. We placed as finalists. We left content from Montreal to go back home.

AERIAL SILKS

MID-JULY TO SEPTEMBER 2011

I was working hard: I was 32 years old and on a mission. The next two months were spent reworking and re-choreographing all of our routines. They needed more spice, so we started working harder. At the same time I continued singing, dancing and studying for my International Latin dance exam. At the end of August I wanted to add another part to my career: the aerial silks. I started training for them the last week of August.

My first lesson was at the Toronto School of Circus Arts. I thought that one day I would be doing tricks on these cool pieces of material high in the air. I soon learned it was bloody hard. I thought I was going to come into this training facility and start climbing to the top, but then I realized it was going to take a lot of time, energy and patience. I was embarrassed on my first lesson because there was a kid's camp taking place on the other side of the gym and I thought the kids would start laughing at me, but they were too busy with their instructor, which made me feel much better.

The next two lessons were at the same place with the kids' camp going on in the background and myself struggling to get up the silks. On the fourth lesson I saw these kids were working in the same area I was. I walked into the gym and thought these kids are going to laugh, but they didn't. At one point I had six little ones from about five to eight years old looking at me. They all gathered around in a semi-circle to see what I was going to do. They were silent and observant. These were the little kid's that had given up and didn't want to climb anymore and so they sat and looked at me. I still couldn't climb on the silks and was struggling, surprisingly enough the kids didn't laugh they simply got up and tried to climb again for the rest of the class. I was so happy, to think I may have inspired them to keep trying and they did.

Finally, on the fifth class I got myself off the ground. I got about a foot off the ground and thought this is going to take a very long time. I was determined to do it no matter how long it would take, I wanted to learn this new art. There were also adult circus artists working at their crafts too, from silks, trapeze, Chinese poles, hoops and more. They inspired me which made me work harder.

NOVEMBER 2011

It's the end of November now and it has been three months since I started climbing the silks. It was hard to find time to train because of my busy schedule, but I managed to fit it in at some point. Most of the time I would sit in afternoon traffic to get to the circus school, but I really wanted to do it, so I would sing to the music on the radio and be on my way.

I can climb up the silks to over one story off the ground now, with some pain in my arms. It wasn't easy. I climbed up and gave myself a five-minute break, just to have a bit of pain relief.

It's been a struggle and I was taking two lessons a week. The administrator, Linda, who was also a trained circus coach, advised me to drop down to one lesson a week because I was complaining of arm pain. She told me I needed more recovery time because I was in pain and just not strong enough yet. I took her advice and went to one lesson a week. It felt better. I needed time to get stronger. Plus, I needed more patience. I really was determined to master this craft. I would dream about this often and in my dreams I had mastered it and was doing shows on a daily basis. Then I would wake up! I knew this wasn't my reality yet: I wasn't even close.

DECEMBER 2011

I was still working hard at everything I have been doing and enjoying it. On the 11th of this month I had a singing recital and I was going to sing *On a Wonderful Day Like today*, from the musical, *The Roar of the Grease Paint and the Smell of the Crowd*. It was a cheerful song, full of happiness and joy. It was a song that best suited my personality, being one of the most enjoyable songs I have ever sung in a long time. I mean, I always loved all the music that I sang and I sang each song with love, passion and excitement.

Plus, I was working and practicing with Mary and we were still in the process of redoing our routines and we hadn't competed in over five months. We should have never stopped competing to completely redo our dance routines. We should have done them one by one and phased out the old ones and slowly added the new routines. That was a mistake that we made.

I was still practicing with Tanya and happy with how that was going. My next dance exam was scheduled for December 22nd. Tanya was a lot of fun. She had a great sense of humour and could deal with my crazy, wacky personality. I was working harder and harder to get this last exam done. Working with her made my life easier; she was easy going and a great teacher and coach. I was reading the dance manuals on a daily basis and dancing around by myself every chance I could get. I would go into the dance studio early on a daily basis, study my dance manuals and go through the dance steps. I would play the music and dance around by myself as if I was performing for a crowd of people.

It was a good break and allowed time for some relaxation while my mind was rejuvenating. I took my exam again with the same examiner, Alan Armsby, and I was so happy to finish my exam.

Now I had my first levels in all four styles across the board, American Rhythm, American Smooth, International Latin and International Standard.

Allan said, "Well done and congratulations on your achievements. You should be very proud of yourself for completing all four styles of dances."

I replied with a huge thank you and added, "Now I know the differences between all four styles." I was so relieved to have these certificates. There are differences between all four styles, but I am not going to bore you to death writing about the differences. Just know that they are different. I was extremely happy and now I was one of the few people in the dancing world in Canada to be certified dancing in all four styles. I worked hard and was ready, once again, as usual I enjoy a Christmas break with good food, partying, fun, family and friends.

BACK TO GREECE

JANUARY, FEBRUARY, MARCH 2012

This Christmas and New Year's Eve were spent with family and friends. I knew the auditions were going to take place soon for *Dancing with the Stars* in Greece and I was looking forward to flying to Greece and participating in the auditions.

I called ENA Productions on January 9th, 2012 and asked when the auditions were going to be taking place. They told me to call back in a week because the date hadn't been set yet. It frustrated me because I needed to book a ticket if I was going to go to an audition at the end of the month. I just waited. I called back on January 15th, 2012 and still a date wasn't set. I was told that it would be sometime at the end of the month or the beginning of February.

I was getting even more frustrated because it's a show that was supposed to be on television in March and we needed a few weeks to rehearse and teach the stars how to dance. I felt they were cutting the time very close.

The stars didn't have any dance experience so they needed to be trained. The other problem was I needed to book my ticket. If I booked a ticket at the last minute, the price can sometimes be doubled. Due to the uncertainty, I had to make a decision and I didn't want to miss the date. I also spoke with Galena in Greece and she told me the production company hadn't put out a date yet. She said she would call me when she found out a definite date.

Eventually I made the decision to book a ticket just to be on the safe side. I found a ticket for $1090 (tax included) and was happy with the price. I was leaving from Toronto on January 22nd arriving the following day. My return date was to be on February 10th. I booked these dates because the audition dates were around the end of January to the beginning of February, so I thought that it would be plenty of time for the production company to make a decision. Plus, I thought it was the logical thing to do since the show was to air in March. I guess I should never have made that assumption.

I arrived in Greece, picked up my rental car and I went straight to Dora's house. I only told a few friends and cousins that I was going to Greece because I was simply sick and tired of listening to people tell me how to run my life and tell me I was doing stuff all wrong and blah, blah, blah.

I felt the need to chase something I really wanted and I was going to do it! That's what I think everybody should do if they really, really, really want their dream to come true. If you don't try, you will never know and as I said before, you can't put a price on peace of mind.

As usual, I was welcomed with open arms by Dora and her family. I only called her and not the rest of my friends in Greece because I wanted to surprise them. Our friends Kelly and Anna were graduating that week with their Masters in Byzantine Archaeology. Dora and I went to their graduation ceremony and they were so surprised. Later I called friends in Athens one by one telling them I was here. They were surprised to hear from me and happy to see that I was chasing my dreams and trying my best to make them reality.

It's now January 28th. I called the production company twice. There still wasn't a set audition date. I was getting frustrated and couldn't understand why there was no date for a show that should be starting less than a month away.

Two days before, I visited the production company. I went through the back door of the company to avoid being told that the producers were busy. I knew that the producer's office was located by the back door, so I thought it was a good idea. I walked in and ran into the producer and gave him my updated resume, with headshots, letters of reference and dancing DVDs of me competing. I told him I was only here in Greece until February 10th and that I came from Canada only for the audition. He said the date hadn't been set yet. I thought to myself this is ridiculous, how can a show so big be put together with so much disorganization? He told me to call back in a week, the classic line I had been hearing since the beginning of January. I said okay, fine, I would call in a week and he said that I would get a phone call too.

The week came and went and again I called a few times in between to see if a date had been set yet. Nobody called me, what else would you expect. I also spoke with Galena and still no date yet. She told me to come to her studio party on Friday night and I said okay.

Now it's February 1st and my departure date was getting closer. I made a decision to stay in Greece for as long as I could for the audition. I thought I would cancel my ticket home. I was tossing and turning every night in my sleep hoping to get a phone call in the morning, every morning. There were many nights where I would wake up in the middle of the night thinking and hoping it was morning so I could get a phone call and then discovered it was 4am and there were plenty of more hours before the sun would come up.

It was crazy. I was in anticipation all the time, sitting and waiting for the phone to ring. Finally, I was told to expect a phone call between 10am to 2pm. I made sure I never left my cell phone unattended. I took it to the washroom with me, I had it with me at every meal, and I just didn't leave my phone alone for one second. I would stare at it for hours hoping it would ring and tell me some good news. It was driving me nuts, waiting and staring and waiting and staring at my phone. In the meantime I was doing nothing, well, I mean I wasn't working while I was in Greece. My friends had jobs and were working and I was just waiting around for the phone to ring. I needed to find something to occupy my time and fast before I went crazy.

It's now 11pm and I had just arrived to the dance studio for open dance night. I paid my entrance fee, walked in and sat down by myself. It was intimidating walking into a place where you don't know a soul. I saw Galena and she greeted me with a warm smile, laughed and made me feel welcomed. I told her how crazy I was going, sitting and waiting by the phone and that I made the decision to stay longer.

She was impressed and told me not to worry, assuring me that all would be fine, just be patient. She told me that the producers go through her and ask her if she has specific dancers to match up with a celebrity because it's not only about dancing, it's about if the couple look good together, in other words the couple should also be visually appealing together. She said she would do whatever it takes to help me get on the show. I proceeded to tell her that I quit everything back home, from work and other commitments just to come and audition for the show. I knew when I went back to Canada I would have to look for work again, but I knew I had the family Greek restaurant, but I didn't want to be a restauranteur for the rest of my life. It just wasn't my dream, not what I wanted in life as a career, it just wasn't for me. She was impressed with my determination. Seeing and speaking with her made me feel fantastic, just to hear some positive conversation was reassuring. It made me feel good because this uncertainty was frustrating. The evening ended on a positive note and I started dancing with students and other teachers and having a good time with all the people at the dance. Everybody was warm and welcoming to me. The open dancing ended at 2am.

It's now February 11th. I cancelled my return flight date on February 10th and I had until July 26th to come home without paying a full price ticket again. I was hoping the audition would be much sooner because I was going to go crazy! I was still calling the production company every few days and I just kept getting the same answer: no audition date was set.

I was told that the show was going to start at the end of March, on the 25th, to be exact so the audition had to be soon, that's what I was thinking in my frustrated mind. The show date changed from the beginning of March to the end of March. Now I was even more frustrated. We have to practice with the stars for at least a month; they need to learn how to dance.

While I was staying in Greece, to make getting around the metropolis of Athens easier, I had rented a car. I had to call the rental company and to extend my car rental because now I was staying longer. I had originally paid 420 Euros for two weeks and I was hoping to get a deal for an extended two weeks. I tried to bargain, but it didn't work. I paid the same amount. I was strapped for money and having a car just made things easier. I just put it on my credit card and would worry about it when I got home to Canada because I didn't want to spend the money that I had.

In the mean time I had to find something to occupy my time. I was going nuts staring at my phone waiting for it to ring so I went on my laptop and searched for a circus school. I found a circus school to train on the aerial silks and do yoga once a week. I met new friends, they were a bunch of crazy artists trying to find new ways of expressing themselves through various art forms. Some were dancers, actors, singers and others were there just out of general interest and had nothing to do with the arts at all, they were working people with normal jobs.

I also found a studio that taught the Argentine tango every Thursday night and they had open tango dancing too. I went and after my first lesson I stayed for open dancing even though I had no clue of what I was doing. I had never taken Argentine tango lessons before.

I would alternate dance partners and drag them around the floor. I just had to give some type of impression that I knew what I was doing, even though I didn't have a clue at all. The Argentine tango was a dance I really wanted to learn, so now was the time.

I was actually told by a few people that I looked good dancing. I was pleasantly surprised and felt better inside, even though I was petrified of learning this new dance. My days were spent doing word searches and socializing with new friends and old friends. I paid a visit to the Acropolis. It was about 0 degrees Celsius, a little cooler for Athens than usual for this time of the year, but it was okay. Well, at least I thought so. I walked to the top of the Acropolis and there were five tourists and me. It was extremely windy and freezing, but great for taking pictures. Visiting there in the summer time was always difficult to take nice photos because it's covered with tourists. Even though it was freezing and windy, it made for nice photos of our Greek ancestor's architecture.

I was looking for a music teacher while I was there, but I figured I had to watch my money as I wasn't working, so I opted not to find a teacher. I went over my vocal warm ups twice a week that I had been doing with my music coach at home and singing through my book of music that I had brought on my own time. Also, every week I was going with my friends Dora's dad to the archaeological society. They were giving weekly lectures about various archaeological topics. I would introduce myself to the speakers and make it known that I was a documentation and archaeological photographer too. Just by chance, I ran into Matt, an old university friend from Canada at the weekly lectures and was so happy and surprised to see him. He was studying at the American Archaeological Institute of Athens completing his PhD. We chatted for a while; exchanged numbers and went out for drinks. It was so awesome to see an old friend from half way across the world.

Now I was busy, I had plenty to do which allowed me to stop staring at my phone for the whole day. Well, I did still stare at my phone, but it was just for half of the day, nevertheless, it made me less frustrated. Even with all this frustration I was having a good time in Athens. Who wouldn't?

Finally, on February 20th, I got a phone call from ENA Productions and was told when the scheduled audition date was going to be. Auditions were to begin Friday February 25th and I was booked in to audition for 1pm on Saturday afternoon.

I arrived early for my audition. I was mentally prepared, found a place to change into my ballroom gear and waited for 1pm to come. Hell, I had been waiting for so long, what's another 40 minutes going to do? They started late and I was not impressed. All the audition times were behind and I went on at 3pm.

One of the dancers in line said to me, "Tasos this is Greece, nothing ever starts on time."

I smiled and started socializing with other dancers. For the audition we had to prepare a one- minute solo ballroom routine and a one-minute solo Latin routine. When I was preparing for my audition, I let my creativity flow. I had plenty of time to think about it. I blended all of my music together. I used four different songs. A friend in Athens, Stavroula, is a computer wizard. She helped me blend the music together using a computer program designed especially to make music cuts; this was wonderful. We used 30 seconds of a waltz, 30 seconds of a tango, 30 seconds of cha cha and 30 seconds of a jive. It was now about 3pm when I went into the room, I greeted the panel of producers and judges, gave a brief introduction of myself then handed my music to the man in charge.

I dressed in my black ballroom three-quarter length jacket, pants and dress shirt. My necktie had 100 Swarovski crystals on it that danced in the light. The music started with the waltz and I sprinkled blue sparkles into the air and went into my self-choreographed routine and then it blended into the tango. Just before the tango routine was over, I took off my jacket and tie and danced over to the side of the room and prepared to go into my cha cha routine and ended the last 30 seconds with my jive routine. It all went by so quickly; it felt like five seconds, yet worth the long wait.

The directors were impressed with what they witnessed. They asked me some general questions, my age and length of my dancing career. They were astounded with the fact that I left everything in Canada to come to Greece for an audition. I was happy with how the question period went. I knew I did my best and I knew deep down inside whatever the outcome, I knew I gave it my all and it was up to them to decide if I was the right fit for the show. Further, I told the panel I had changed my travel plans and I asked when I would know if I was going to be on the show or not. They told me I should know by the end of the week or so. I said thank you to the panel, went to my bag and pulled out a small broom and dustpan and swept up the sparkles on the floor. The panel loved it and laughed with me as I was cleaning up. I left the studio feeling full of excitement and with butterflies in my stomach. I went to my friend's place and told her the news in great detail. She smiled and was happy for me.

The end of the week came and went which also meant it was the end of February too. There was no answer from the production company. I called the following week and asked if there was any decision made and they told me no. I was so frustrated. Once again I was waiting by the phone every day, hoping it would ring with great news of being on the show. I was told that I would get a phone call between 2pm and 4pm. I hung up the phone and felt like screaming my head off. At least the time frame was much smaller than it was before; this time it was only a two-hour time bracket rather than most of the day.

Now it was March and the anticipation was making me crazy. I was back to not sleeping at night because of all of the anticipation of wanting to know the answer. I was on pins and needles for almost three weeks. I held my phone in my hand like it was the Holy Bible on Sunday or better yet like a beer on an evening of socializing with friends from 2pm to 4pm every day from Monday to Friday in hopes it was going to ring.

I had just celebrated my 33rd birthday and it was fun while waiting for an answer! I called again around March 12th and they told me to be on standby. They didn't give me an answer, but they did express it was going to be a positive outcome and would be promising. I told her I was here almost two months now. She told me I had every right to be upset with the disorganization of the show. It didn't matter how upset or full of craziness I was full of inside, it still didn't change the fact that I hadn't received an answer yet.

On Friday March 16th, in the evening, I was sitting around thinking this week of waiting was over and I was in for a new week of waiting the following Monday. It was 8:30pm, and my phone rang and it was the production company. It was the same woman I had been communicating with over the past little while.

I was so excited to hear from her and was expecting fantastic news. I thought the answer is finally here and had butterflies in my stomach again. The time had finally come. She asked me how I was doing and I said I was fine, but then the unexpected happened: she told me the show had been cancelled.

My emotions turned to disappointment. She told me the network couldn't afford to run the show, they had *Greece Has Talent* and *Dancing with the Stars* at the same time and there wasn't enough in the budget to run both shows at the same time. So the network opted to choose *Greece Has Talent* because they had started filming it.

Even though I was disappointed, I was relieved because I finally had an answer. It was time to go home and continue working toward my goals; the road didn't end here for me. I booked my ticket home for March 26th. I spent the next week saying goodbye to my friends. They all told me that they admired me for chasing what I wanted in life. I told them I wasn't giving up, even though I was disappointed. Anyway, I enjoyed the time I had spent with my friends, they were extremely supportive as all my friends were back home and all over the world.

BACK TO THE DRAWING BOARD

APRIL 2012 TO MAY 2012

I had been home for about two weeks now and took this time to tell all my family and friends about what happened in Greece. They were all disappointed for me and I appreciated it, but as I told my friends in Greece, I wasn't stopping. I had worked so hard to get to this point and now I was driven more than ever. I told the story many, many, many times and by the end of these two weeks I was done talking about it.

I went back to my circus training, back to the gym and singing lessons. My singing coach Roland was so good to me. He knew I was in a bind and believed in me; therefore, he gave me a few lessons for free. I continued with my ballroom and Latin dance coach too.

One thing I neglected to do while I was away all that time was to make contact with my dance partner Mary. I was going to via email or Facebook, but I didn't. I made very little contact with anybody for that matter. It was my mistake. I was so preoccupied and focused on trying to make contact with the show that I just wasn't thinking normally. My mind was all over the place. I was in Greece for one reason and I had worked so hard to get to that point, but nevertheless, I should have made some contact.

I called her and it went straight to her voice mail. I apologized and said I was sorry and I meant it. I didn't hear from her.

At this point I decided to get an agent that would represent me in all of my talents. It had been over seven years since I had been in theatre and I found a theatre company in Hamilton. It was community theatre and I decided to join Shooting Star Theatrics. I auditioned for *Annie Get Your Gun* and I got the role of Tommy Keeler. I felt it was time to do some theatre. The rehearsals started weekly and they were two to three times a week at the beginning and as time went on the days increased.

About one year earlier I was working at our family restaurant (as I often did on the weekends) and a tall lady in her 30s came in for dinner. I was chatting with her and she told me she owned a talent agency. She gave me her card and told me to give her a call, but I never followed through with it. I kept her card on my dresser and looked at it from time to time and wondered what it would be like to have an agent. Finally, I gave her a call, I asked for her specifically and I described who I was and she remembered me. She called me in for an interview and was happy to put me onto their talent roster. She gave me the address of the photographer that they used and I went in for some headshots. I also forwarded my resume and within two weeks I was going to multiple auditions, from everything from commercials to print ads to short films.

While I was in Greece I would get bored and I surfed the Internet trying to find myself a new skill to take up. I was on YouTube one day and I typed in "fire tricks". Don't ask me how I came up with that I idea. I just did. I watched multiple videos on fire poi, fire spinning. Two chains are held, one in each hand, and they are about a foot long each with wicks at each end. You would light them on fire and start doing tricks, but it wasn't that easy. Then I did a google search and found a company named "Home of Poi" and I ordered all the equipment and a DVD and had it sent to my home in Canada from New Zealand.

When I would go to the gym I took my laptop, fire poi equipment and the DVD and spent three hours every night for about four weeks in the aerobics room from 9pm to midnight and got myself to an intermediate level. It was show worthy I might add. The room was empty at that time, so I just walked in and used it. Sometimes people would walk in to stretch and warm up; they'd look at me in awe as I bashed my head and my man parts trying to learn how to spin this equipment. Oh, and one other thing, I never lit the ends on fire until I was ready and confident to do so — and of course it was done outdoors in the evening when you could see the fire in its full effect.

JUNE 2012

Now I was working at everything on a daily basis and enjoying it very much. Finally, I got a text message from Mary, my former dance partner. It was nice and polite, I could tell that she was upset with me because it took her over six weeks to reply. She candidly said, "I am glad you are alive and welcome home." I texted back and said we should get together at some point. She agreed. I was disappointed that it took six weeks for her to return my message, but I created the situation, so I shouldn't be upset in fairness to her. We never did make any arrangements to get together again. I sent a few sporadic messages via Facebook and texts, but it didn't seem like she was interested anymore. I understood she was upset and I just let the communication fizzle too. It was my mistake as well. I just left it; anyway, it was fun dancing with her and maybe we'll run into each other at some point in life again. I wish her well at whatever she chooses to do.

At this time it was the middle of June. I called Mary Claude Vincent, from *Cirque du Soleil* because she had gave me her contact information in case I had any questions. I called and described who I was from last year: the crazy ballroom dancer that came to drill her with questions.

She laughed and said she did remember and was delighted to speak with me. I told her I was in the process of making a DVD of me singing, dancing and doing fire poi. I further told her I was going to drive to Montreal to give my DVD in person. She said it wasn't necessary. I said it was because I was so interested in working with the company that I had to do whatever it took to get onto their database of artists. Their database was a very hard database to get on to; they only take one to two percent of people who apply. I really needed to make an impression with this company. So I was willing to do whatever it took.

JULY 2012

Everything was going great, my work, working on mastering my talents and the theatre production. While I was working on everything I would search the internet for auditions all over North America. I came across a website that posted auditions for Broadway productions in New York City. I thought to myself, I would love to go on Broadway, what a dream. The audition I came across was for *Phantom of the Opera*. It was under the Equity Actors Union. You see, large productions such as this one were always posted as union jobs and I wasn't part of the union. To be part of the union you needed to find two theatre companies and do three plays that offered an apprenticeship under the actors union. Getting one of those jobs was hard, but not impossible. I called the union and asked if I should go to New York. They strongly suggested that there was no point in going, but I went anyway. They did say that sometimes, depending on the director, they would put up audition sign-up sheets for non-union members, but it was very rare.

I drove down to New York City on a Thursday night and found the cheap hotel I booked online in Times Square. It was a nine-hour drive and just after 9pm when I settled into the hotel and then walked around New York for a few hours. The audition was at Pearl Studios just down the street from the hotel, about a 15-minute walk from Times Square. The audition was scheduled at 11am the next morning. I woke up, got dressed, put my best clothes on, had some breakfast and proceeded to walk to the studios. I arrived and there was a sign-in sheet for union members and there was a sign-in sheet for non-union members. You don't know until you try. I handed in my resume to the person in charge and I was told to come back at 2pm. There were over 50 guys that were non-union and about 100 guys that belonged to the union. I came back and my resume was handed back to me, which means they didn't pick me. At least I tried and I got my answer. It was my first experience in a New York City audition and at least I got a feel for what was going on in New York. Now I could go home and continue working on my craft.

SHOWTIME

AUGUST 2012

It was now the beginning of the month and the show dates weren't too far away. The cast had been working extremely hard to move forward with ups and downs along the way. It got intense at times because people were getting nervous and ironing out various details before the show was ready to go on stage. While all this was happening, I was still teaching in the evenings when we didn't have practice and I was still working at the family restaurant, singing and all the other fun stuff I did.

My schedule was all over the place as usual, but I made it work and things were getting done in all aspects. The show dates were August 17th at 8pm; 18th at 2pm and at 8pm; 24th at 8pm; 25th at 8pm; and the final show was on the 26^{th,} at 2pm.

It had been years since I had been on a stage. To tell you the truth, I was a little nervous and excited at the same time. It's good to be nervous; it keeps you on your toes and alert, that way you don't get too comfortable. I had a big part so I had to be ready. The one thing I didn't miss about doing theatrical productions was the thick "cakey" make-up that we had to wear.

It was like putting toothpaste on your face and letting it dry. Well, okay, okay it wasn't that bad, but I didn't like it. We did our own make-up every night, well at least I did, and then we all helped each other to put our microphones on using clear body tape to stick to the side of our faces.

The last time I was in a show, microphones weren't being used, we had to project our voices. I felt it took away from the whole feeling of using projection and was replaced by technology. People told me that this was becoming the norm and has been for years. Gee, I wonder where I was when this was happening, probably on some dreamy cloud. In any case, I still loved it and was looking forward to the show.

It was opening night. I was pacing back and forth and getting myself ready to go on stage and into character. From time to time I would peek through the big heavy curtains and see the house starting to fill up with people. I sold over 50 tickets and for each show there would be somebody I knew in the audience. The orchestra started to play and it was amazing. The cast gathered back stage and quietly waited for the musical cue to tell us when to come on stage to do our opening number. This was the biggest number of the show with all 40 cast members on stage.

The musical cue came up and we all entered the stage from different areas singing and dancing. I heard my cue and I walked on stage singing. I felt so alive, so full of life and I gave every last fiber of my being to belt out my lines in the opening number. The rush felt like I was on a roller coaster and screaming at the top of my lungs, well I didn't scream, but I sure felt alive. I just got lost in my character and was full of so much fulfillment that I enjoyed every last second I was on stage with the cast. We all fed off of each other's energy and supported each other every step of the way. It was exciting to say the least.

At the end of each show we received applause that sounded like thunder roaring through the theatre. People were screaming of joy and happiness, others whistled and the crowd was on their feet with amazement. I loved the fact that we, as a cast, made the audience enjoy what they saw. It was truly a great feeling. As we exited the stage we were high-fiving each other and applauding each other for the amazing work we all did. We went back stage to the dressing rooms and changed and then we would go and greet our families and friends in the lobby. They had flowers and gifts for us; it was fantastic!

During one of our shows a couple of theatre critics were present. We didn't know, but they came and congratulated us after our show and said we had done an amazing job. They were from the Ontario Arts Council.

The next day they wrote a review raving that we were one of the top ten musical community theatre groups in Ontario: it was a huge compliment. They loved the fact that we had so many costume changes to compensate for the lack of setting on stage. In community theatres, budgets are low and so they make do with what they have and we did a great job according to the critic.

I received an amazing compliment from the council. The critic wrote that my number, *Who Do You Love, I hope,* was the show stopping number. I was so happy and as I was reading the review that had been posted in the hallway of our dressing rooms, my eyes welled up with tears of happiness. It was such a great feeling to receive such a great compliment. It felt like I was doing something right. All of my hard work over the years was paying off to some degree and I was so happy and overwhelmed with joy.

The show came to an end and it all went very well. The entire cast worked extremely hard to be in character at all times to put on a good show. We all assisted in taking the set down and taking it back to the studio and cleaned up the theatre. It ended with a cast party with pizza, cake and a lot of great junk food. We all were complimenting each other for a great job we had all done on stage. Others were giving hugs, some were giving handshakes and others were just plain crying of joy. Hey! We're in acting so of course we are going to have a drama king and queen that are going to cry at the end of the show. The director thanked everyone and stated it was a pleasure working with us and complimented us on having done a fabulous job.

When it was all over, I got into my car and had a moment before I left. I just stared into the distance and felt so happy with what we all had done. I just loved being on stage performing and I wanted to do more.

The last week of August I was approached by a cast member to audition for another community theatre group. I told her I wasn't sure because I was waiting to hear from *Dancing with the Stars* in Greece. The production company said the show was going to run in the fall and they said they were going to call me. Regardless, I went to the audition and told the director and crew that I was waiting to hear from *Dancing with the Stars* in Greece and that I should know by September 15th if the show was going to run. They really appreciated my honesty. I was cast as part of the chorus and they told me to start rehearsing. Just in case the show wasn't going to run, at least I would be familiar with the music and the stage blocking. I agreed because they were very accommodating.

GOING BACK TO THE HEAD OFFICE OF CIRQUE DU SOLEIL

SEPTEMBER 2012

I called Mary Claude from *Cirque du Soleil* the first week of September and I made an appointment to drive to Montreal the second Monday of September to hand in my DVD to the company. I called a good friend of mine, Suzanna, who lives in Montreal and asked if I could stay with her for a few days.

I told her why I was coming to Montreal and she loved the idea and was happy for me. I left Sunday morning and drove about six hours to Montreal. I arrived early in the evening and Suzanna had given me her apartment all to myself. She was going to stay at her boyfriend's house so I could have my own space and privacy, which was just awesome and extremely accommodating. She hid the key of her apartment in a special spot and texted me instructions were to find it. I found the key and let myself into to her apartment. I was greeted with a welcome note on the kitchen table telling me to make myself at home and help myself to any food in the house, so I did. Also she gave me a phone number where I could contact her and we would meet up at some point for breakfast or lunch.

I called her when I arrived and we met up the next morning for breakfast. She came down to the apartment and we greeted each other with a great big hug and went for breakfast. I told her in detail what my plan was for the day, she laughed and told me she loved the idea.

After breakfast she went on with her day and I with mine. I walked to the subway station, boarded the train and was off to *Cirque du Soleil's* head office. It was a warm sunny day; I got off at the Jean Talon Station again and walked to the head office just as I did one year ago. I finally arrived at the headquarters and asked to speak with Mary Claude. She came down and greeted me. I handed her nine silver envelopes and I asked if she could hand my package out to the people in charge. She said yes. I asked if I could meet any of the scouts or if anybody was available.

Mary Claude called a few of the people in the building and said a woman by the name of Estelle Esse was available. She came to the front desk to greet me and I handed her one of my silver packages. She took it and held it in her arms. Then I got down straight to business and asked if I could ask her a few questions about the company and how it operates. I just wanted to learn anything I could.

My first question was, "How long does it take to get into *Cirque du Soleil?*"

She replied, "It could take up to a few weeks or a few years, once you have been accepted in the database of artists."

I know they only accept one to two percent of people for a general audition of any of the disciplines. Then they pick from the database of artists that they think you would be best suited for a role. Then you get called in for an audition for a specific part (singer, dancer, actor, acrobatics, extreme sports etc.).

Estelle was extremely friendly and answered my questions with detail. After my questions, they proceeded to give me a small tour of the headquarters. I was excited, but didn't show it. Well, okay, okay, I did show it. I had a huge smile on my face, like a child on Christmas morning who got the toy he wanted all year long. I had to contain myself and not start jumping up and down, but my heart was pounding with excitement.

They showed me a training facility, a large gym where part of the set was up for the artists that were training for *Dralion* a touring show. In another part of the gym was a huge swing in the shape of a long boat suspended from the ceiling that looked like it held five to ten people and artists were training for *O* the permanent water show in Las Vegas playing at the Bellagio. We continued on to the practice rooms, one had a piano and this was where the singer would practice and prepare for a show. All the music in *Cirque du Soleil* is performed live.

As we were going into these rooms, the hallways were lined with closets, door after door after door. Mary Claude told me that all these closets were full of costumes from past shows. They were kept for the possibility of using them for another show. I asked if we could look inside, she said yes. I was excited again and as I mentioned before, it doesn't take much for me to get excited: I was up in the stars! She proceeded to open a door and it was full of colour: neon pink and green and all kinds of colours in all kinds of material, from lycra to cotton and everything in between. It was simply awesome! I was told the company makes all the costumes right here at headquarters.

We then proceeded to a massive warehouse and I mean massive. It looked like it was 40, 000 square feet of empty space. Once the show had been created they would build the show in this area and run it before it goes on tour or to its permanent location. They really do everything here; every last detail is created at headquarters. What an amazing production. We ended off the tour at the cafeteria, where they had a very healthy menu for its artists and staff.

The tour lasted an hour or so and Estelle asked, "Why didn't you just apply online? It would have been easier and saved you a trip and time."

I replied, "I know a lot of people want to get into this company and I am aware that you get hundreds of applications, or even thousands from all over the world on a weekly basis. I have to prove myself to somebody here that I want to really work for *Cirque du Soleil*. I have to stand out and be different! And I believe this is how it's done, you get to see me and get to know who I am and what I represent as a person and an artist."

They were both taken back when I was done with my answer. They put out their hands for a shake; I gave them a bear hug instead. They laughed and we said goodbye. I waved as I left the building and left fulfilled. I went back to my friend's apartment, we caught up some more, had a great dinner and many, many laughs. The next day, in the mid-morning, I got up and drove back home to Hamilton.

WAITING

MID-SEPTEMBER 2012

It was now the middle of the month and no news whatsoever from *Dancing with the Stars* in Greece. I was disappointed because I really wanted to be on the show and if it starts in October, as they said it would, then I didn't get a call. Good God, I was starting to think the waiting game was going to start happening all over again. I really didn't want to go through all that again. Deep down inside I was ready to do it all over again, ready to wait. I was preparing myself mentally to feel the same way as I did at the beginning of the year. I went to the community theatre company and spoke with the director. I told him that I was going to back out of the show, stay home and wait for that special phone call from Greece. I didn't want to put anybody out or make people's lives difficult so I thought backing out was the best and fair thing to do. I knew they had a show to run. The director wanted me to stay and said we would cross that bridge when we came to it. I appreciated his understanding. I said thank you and went on my way to rehearsal and learned the script along with the other chorus members twice a week.

It was now the end of September and there was still no word from *Dancing with the Stars*. I couldn't believe this, if the show was going to start in October we needed to start teaching the stars some type of dancing so they would be prepared.

It was the same song and dance all over again, but this time I was in the comfort of my own home, which made for an easier time because I could go about my day as usual. This roller coaster of emotions started to get to me after a while, one being happy, and one being in anticipation, one being down, up and down and up and down. I just kept waiting.

As I was waiting I did get some other fantastic news. I received an email from *Cirque du Soleil*. It was an official email. I opened my email, it was a certificate lined in sunshine yellow that read, "Congratulations you have now been put on the data base of artists."

I was retained as a multi-disciplinarian, a singer, dancer, actor and fire spinner. I read the letter in disbelief and started crying of happiness. I read the email a multiple of times to see if what I was reading was true or not. It really was, I was on the database of artists. Wow! In my industry, it is one of the hardest things in the world to attain and I was now on it. I couldn't believe my eyes, it took so much hard work and it was starting to pay off even more. I called my parents, I called all of my friends and cousins and everybody else I knew and every Greek person for that matter. I was so happy. I was gleaming with joy. Everybody I told was extremely happy for me and was just over joyed with emotion. At least something went well this month. It was a great piece of news and it brought my spirits up.

OCTOBER 2012

I was still practicing fire spinning a few times a week at the gym, of course without fire. I'd take my laptop and my DVD to learn and practice fire tricks as often as I could. I was still hitting myself in the head and my man parts as I learned new tricks, but in any case, I was getting better and better at this new artistic craft. I was still training on the circus silks and it seemed like it wasn't getting any easier. It was really hard, but I didn't want to give it up. At night I was still dreaming about how I was doing shows in my dreams, but it wasn't a reality yet.

I get an unexpected phone call at 11am on October 19th. It was Friday and I was still sleeping because I didn't have to work until late afternoon. I had a weird schedule. Some days I worked until 11pm and other days until 6pm, it varied. From time to time I would go salsa dancing with my friend Farrah (which is what I did the night before) it was great, and hence why I slept in.

Anyway, the call was from Greece. It was one of the director's assistants. I was taken by surprise and jumped out of bed. I was asked, if the show ran, would I still want to participate in the show. I said yes, yes, yes with plenty of enthusiasm. I told them I needed to know before Tuesday if I was going to be on the show or not, not by Tuesday I said — before Tuesday. The assistant director was shocked and asked why so early? This Greek style of working sometimes makes you crazy and makes you laugh at the same time. I told them that if the show happened, I would have to leave a theatre group: one that was very accommodating and one that I was most grateful to. Plus, I had to make arrangements for somebody to cover my dance classes at various locations and I needed to pack. The assistant agreed and told me that someone would call me "before" Tuesday. Well they didn't. What else is new?

They called me Tuesday morning at 11am. I was practically making love to my cell phone at night because I didn't want to miss an important call from Greece. I had it on my night table and the night table was pulled as close as possible to my bed. I recreated the same behaviour that I was doing in Greece. I took my cell phone everywhere with me: to the washroom, to bed, to work -everywhere! It didn't leave my side at all.

Well, the phone rang at the perfect time, while I was singing in the shower. I had the phone on the bathroom sink, which was in arms reach from the shower. I quickly turned off the shower and answered the phone dripping wet and naked. I sat there with chills running up and down my body for a few moments until I managed to put the phone on speaker and set it on the sink while I grabbed for the towel.

It was the assistant director and he asked, "Are you ready for some great news?"

I said, "Yes."

He said, "Leave everything behind and come be a professional dancer on *Dancing with the Stars* Greece! What's your answer?"

I said very loudly, "Yes, yes, yes, I want to be on the show!"

I was jumping for joy! After all this waiting and going back and forth to Greece, I finally had an answer. I was going to be on the show. I was so excited I just sat on the bathroom floor for a moment to gather my thoughts. I was so overwhelmed with happiness that finally after all my hard work and perseverance I was going to be on the show that I had tried so hard to get on for the past two years. What a feeling.

The assistant director then asked me if I could be in Greece by tomorrow. I said, "I am not coming from across the street or the other side of Athens for that matter." I was coming from half way across the world with a seven hour time difference and I had a nine hour flight too. I said I needed a few days. He laughed and said that was fine and that he understood.

I went to a travel agency and booked a ticket to fly out of Toronto on Thursday evening. Then I had to tell the theatre company that I was leaving. I figured it wouldn't be a problem, since the director already knew the situation. I called my friends and family from Hamilton to Greece and shared my news. I called both Greek communities in Hamilton and the priests told me they would make an announcement after church on Sunday. I also called the Greek community in St. Catherine's and the largest Greek community in Toronto, Panagia Greek Orthodox church because I knew the priest there too. He was once the parish priest in Hamilton, Ontario, where I live and grew up.

Just a side note, Greek communities outside of Greece and all over the world have community centres with the church attached to them; hence, why I called the church and clergy. Now it was time to go to the community theatre company.

It was now 7pm. I left my house anxious of how I was going to tell the director I was leaving his show to participate on *Dancing with the Stars*. I didn't think it would be a problem. In September when I wanted to leave he told me to stay and if I needed to go, we would cross that bridge when we got to it.

I thought our meeting would go smoothly. I arrived at the theatre company at around 6:15pm. I was nervous telling him, but I knew he would understand because he was informed. I pulled into the parking lot and waited for him. He arrived a few minutes later. I got out of my car and so did he. I approached him and said that I had something to say to him, he nodded his head, indicating for me to speak.

I told him *Dancing with Stars* was a go and that I had been working for a very long time to get onto the show in Greece. He was upset and told me that at this point in time he didn't think the show in Greece was a go ahead.

I said sorry and I hoped he'd understand. He then proceeded to say, "I understand that it's a career advancement for you, but you have a reputation to keep up, whether it was amateur or professional."

I was so disappointed because I told him at two different points that I wanted to leave the show and wait at home for a potential call and he told me to stay with the theatre group and not to worry. I was expecting a totally different reaction. I told him. I was upfront with him from the beginning.

He told me to come into the theatre. He was going to tell the assistant director, choreographer, and stage manager. I was sitting around waiting and it was almost 6:50pm in the evening. I saw a few cast members that I had told before that I was trying to be on

Dancing with the Stars. I told them I was leaving and they were so happy for me, they wished me well and good luck.

Finally, the choreographer said to come and meet them in a separate room. She gave me a hug and told me she understood, but she was upset too. She smiled and told me, "You need to do what is right for you."

Then she gave me another smile and said that the assistant director wants you to leave the building. I laughed and so did she, but not too loud. We went into the room and if looks could kill I would so be dead. I said I was sorry and told them flat out I couldn't give up this opportunity. She was upset. They all were very upset.

I was upset that the director didn't speak up and say that he had a part in this too. Both times he told me to stay when I approached him about leaving the show. I didn't want to stay because I was trying to avoid this situation from happening and he didn't say anything at all. That wasn't fair. I told him privately on two occasions that I wanted to leave and wait at home for a possible phone call from Greece. The rest of the crew didn't know that we spoke. They all probably assumed I just did this out of the blue. He just stood there in silence, not speaking at all.

They all told me to leave because they had a rehearsal. I said okay, but before I left I wanted to tell the cast members myself that I was leaving the show. They said no and that they would take care of it. I understood why they were upset. Regardless, I approached them and offered them a handshake and thanked them for all of their work. Reluctantly, they shook my hand. The director reminded me as I shook his hand that I have a reputation to up keep and it's up to me to keep it going. I was thinking the same thing about him. It just wasn't fair that he didn't say a thing. They whole thing looked like I left without a care in the world about the show. I did, in fact, care. I was very clear from the beginning and now I looked like I was the bad guy. It's my fault too, I should have spoken up. I should have said something and I didn't. I should have pointed out that the director knew what was going on. I was just too afraid because I felt like I was cornered by a group of people, it was me against them. Here is my advice to you. If you are in a situation like I was, speak up and voice your opinion when you know something is not right.

The next day I got a call from a cast member and I explained the situation and how it all panned out. I further explained that I wanted to tell the cast on my own, but I was told to leave the theatre. He said the crew of the show told the cast, but my friend wanted to hear it from me. I did what I could by the end of all of this. I was honest from the beginning and did my very best. It didn't turn out how I expected it to turn out, but I guess you just live and learn.

I was on my way home now and I was preparing for my trip to Greece. I spent the next few days packing for the show. I packed all my dance shoes and my dance clothes too. My friend Eleni took me to the airport, she bought me lunch too at the airport and sent me off on my way to Greece. It was a hard few days, but I managed. All was going very well now; I was off to Greece.

FINALLY: DANCING WITH THE STARS GREECE.

FRIDAY, OCTOBER 26, 2012

I woke up this morning and stared at the ceiling thinking in utter disbelief that my dream finally came true. After all of my hard work, waiting and waiting, emotions of all kinds, sad and happy, going off like fireworks.

I had this big grin on my face as I pulled the covers off, got out of bed and started my day. I walked around my room going in and out of drawers, my closet and making sure that I hadn't forgotten to add anything to my luggage. Then, I made my way to my suitcase to zip it up and bring it to the front door of my house. I spent that day taking care of loose ends at work. I needed to make sure I had a neat and tidy room for when I return from this fantastic adventure. I made my way to the airport wondering if I brought everything I needed. I can't believe this is happening was going over and over in my head. I checked my luggage, went through customs and boarded my evening flight to Greece.

I arrived in Greece at 5pm the next day and it was warm outside. I made my way outside from the airport to be greeted by a long line up of yellow taxis waiting to take tourists and local Greeks to their final destinations. I got in a taxi and informed the driver that I would be staying at the Titania Hotel in the centre of Athens.

It's a five star hotel with a white marble lobby with a grand piano to the side of the main entrance. It was like a dream, well it was reality. I had never stayed in such a nice hotel in my life. I am a budget traveller staying in pensions, hostels and campsites, so this was a treat for me. I went to the front desk and informed the person in charge that I was here to check in and a professional dancer that will be participating on *Dancing with the Stars*. I was given a room key and told to go to the top floor of the hotel.

I got off the elevator and went to my room. It was beautiful and the most amazing part of the room was the view: I had a spectacular view of the Acropolis. It was just simply incredible, it was so close to my window that I felt I could just reach out and touch it. After I was done getting acquainted with my room, my phone rang and I was asked to call the studios.

I called Alexia (she was the young woman that I was dealing with on the phone from Canada) and she was extremely helpful. She gave me directions on how to get to the studio to meet and greet with the producers and staff at some point over the next few days. She told me to relax and get adjusted to the time change in Greece and enjoy my weekend because on Monday morning, everything will start happening with the show. I spent the weekend calling friends and relatives and visiting them too.

Everybody was excited for me and happy that I was going to be on television and so was I.

MONDAY, OCTOBER 29, 2012

I got up early to take the metro to Marousi, a suburb of Athens. From there I transferred to a bus and got off at Ziridi Avenue and walked about three blocks to ENA Productions. I arrived and asked to speak with Alexia. I got to her office, knocked on the door and I was greeted by a group of people smoking and having their coffee. I love Greece. She greeted me and made me feel at home.

My appointment was scheduled for noon and I arrived at 11:30am. I waited in the office making small talk with other staff members. At about 12:15pm, the director, a husky looking guy with salt and pepper hair who was holding a cigarette in his hand too, greeted me. We spoke for about an hour and a half about life, what was going to happen on the show and who my star was going to be. He matched me with this particular star because she was outgoing, happy and social, just like I was. He told me I didn't look like a dancer last winter when I came for the audition; he said I looked like a football player or a boxer because I was a built guy.

Afterward, I was laughing inside because I didn't have a clue about either sport. He also added last March that his decision was made after about ten seconds of meeting me. He and the crew felt my personality was perfect for the show. They loved everything from my dancing right down to my disposition.

That afternoon around 5:30pm I met my star, my dance partner for the show. We started chatting and getting to know each other. The camera crew was at the studio during our "meet and greet" and I was getting to know them too. Everybody was friendly, warm, welcoming and extremely accommodating as well. Her manager was there too, who was her boyfriend.

The show was scheduled to premiere November 11th, 2012. The next few days were spent teaching her how to ballroom and Latin dance. Our first dance was the cha cha. Slowly, I started to show her the basic style and movement of the cha cha and the basic steps and then we moved into the choreography for the show.

She was getting a lot of negative attention in the media because she was a trained ballet dancer. The point of the show is to have celebrities that didn't have any dance knowledge and they were to come to the show and learn how to dance. She didn't seem bothered by the negative attention in the media and I wasn't either, well, I mean it had nothing to do with me anyway.

After she learned the basics of the cha cha, and I was starting to teach her the choreography, she was slowly trying to take over the composition. I was being extremely patient and allowing her to give some input, but she just wanted to do it all.

On Wednesday, October 31st I received a friendly phone call from the director suggesting that I should let her join in on the choreography. I said I was letting her. He asked, "Can you then let her do some more?"

I agreed. At our next practice I told her she could choreograph the last 20 seconds of the routine, she agreed and was happy. We continued dancing over the next few days working hard at what we were doing, but more and more she wanted to take over the entire choreography and wanted to add dance moves that had nothing to do with ballroom and Latin dancing.

When you do show routines you do add elements of your own creativity between the designated steps to add some more flare, but she was getting to the point of not using any basic cha cha steps at all. I was now becoming the student and she the teacher. I politely said to her that this is a ballroom and Latin dance show and those are the rules, I was following traditional instruction.

I gave her an inch and then was told to give her another inch and she just took a mile, more than a mile. We weren't arguing, but I had to stop it, or it wasn't going to look like a cha cha routine in the end. I was just doing my job and doing what I was told.

In the evenings, after we had the day to practice with our designated stars, the dance professionals met at a studio where we were being taught the choreography for the show's opening number. We usually met after 10pm so there was plenty of time to make my way from wherever I was in Athens to the designated studio. It was the first time I had danced with other professional dancers in a formation. We all worked hard after an already long day and by the end of the session we were all exhausted, but pushed ourselves because of the love for dance.

NOVEMBER 4, 2012

Today I had to be at Studio Kappa. This main studio is where a lot of famous movies and shows were filmed in Greece; it's just outside of Athens. It was an amazing feeling to be on the grounds where famous Greek stars of the past and present had worked.

I had never been in such a setting of that size ever in my life. I had to be there in the afternoon. I entered the studio and was greeted by Alexia and other staff members of the production company. Alexia showed me to the main hall where the set for *Dancing with the Stars* was being built. We walked in and I was in awe. With the sounds of hammers and drills there were workers everywhere making this lavish set come to life. I had firework displays of happiness going on inside my body as my heart pounded with delight. After the exciting visit to the set, I was taken to a dressing room where I was going to get ready for the afternoon. I brought my black dance pants, black sequined three-quarter length sleeved shirt with a long V-neck to wear and shoes for the afternoon.

Once I was ready, I proceeded to get my make-up done. I sat in this comfortable black chair and was greeted by a friendly make-up artist. I sat and stared at the long, long counter full of make-up of all colours and shades and above the long counter was a mirror the same length with lights around the perimeter.

I was doing a dance routine of happiness inside, staring at myself in the mirror and saying in my head, "You are finally here." My eyes welled up with tears and the make-up artist asked me if I was okay. I said yes, I just said it was the eye make-up that was bothering my eyes, she smiled and continued doing her job with delight.

Now I was ready. I was brought to the main studio and put in front of a camera and asked to tell a little bit about myself and how much I loved dancing. Then I was brought into another area where there was a green screen and was told to do a few dance moves; this was going to be added to my introduction of the show. The directors made me feel at home and comfortable and let's not forget they were all smoking, I love the "chill" kind of attitude in Greece. It was truly a different way of life than I was used to back home in Canada.

I was trying so hard to concentrate and listen to the staff and not show my emotions. I just wanted to start doing cartwheels all over the place. We did all the necessary interviews and then I was directed to the photographer. He took pictures of me doing various dance poses and then together with my partner. The day went really well. I was overwhelmed with sheer excitement of this new adventure and looking forward to it, second by second, minute by minute to the premiere of the show.

A SURPRISE

MONDAY NOVEMBER 5, 2012

I slept in today because of the busy past few days. I woke up at around 10:30am and admired the view of the Acropolis from my bed. I finally got up at 11am, had a shower and was taking my time because I was going to meet my star for practice at 3pm.

I had plenty of time to get ready, get something to eat and start my day. As I was styling my hair in the bathroom I heard the phone ring. I wiped my hands on the towel and ran to the telephone. It was Alexia. She told me to come down to the main office in Maroussi. I told her that I had taping and dancing with my star at 3pm. She said don't worry about that and I said okay.

I was excited because the director had told me during our meet and greet that there might be a possibility to use my singing talent at some point during the show. In other words, I sing and a professional couple would dance, how super cool!

I was told to come down to the office for 2pm, there was something the director wanted to say to me. The transportation was running late. Due to the financial crisis in Greece there were a lot of strikes taking place, one day the buses were on strike, another the taxis, and another day all methods of transportation were on strike. Today the buses were running, thank God, but the traffic in Athens was just unbelievable.

I was only familiar with the subway system in Athens, but they were on strike. I was in luck, my friend Foti worked a five-minute walk from my hotel, which was great. I called him for help and he came over to my hotel to walk me to the specific town square to catch the right bus. I was so relieved because I was about to panic. I didn't know where I was going.

I boarded the bus and the journey took about an hour and 35 minutes, when it should have taken only 35 minutes. The city was in utter chaos, jam packed buses were everywhere, cars, mopeds everything was at a halt, bumper to bumper traffic and nobody was moving. To add to it all, it was hot outside and people were shoving and pushing to get onto the buses that were already packed with passengers. People were arguing with drivers, because they were full to capacity and not allowed on. Cars were honking, people were yelling and frustration was everywhere.

I finally arrived at my bus stop, got off and walked about ten minutes at a steady pace to the production company office. I was excited and looking forward to hearing some more positive news and walked as briskly as possible. I arrived at the office, was greeted by the receptionist smoking a cigarette and asked to speak with the director. I was directed to his office with my heart pounding with excitement and anticipation. I saw him waiting outside of his door and I greeted him with a friendly hello and he the same.

He said to me in English with a thick Greek accent, "I have bad news to tell you."

I was taken back, my heart pounded, but this time with fear of not knowing what to expect. With shock in my voice I asked, "What?"

He then responded in a voice with despair and disappointment, "You can't continue on the show."

I was even more shocked and asked, "Why?"

He couldn't give me a straight answer and I could tell he was beating around the bush. He was probably trying to formulate some type of reason in his head on how to tell me the awful news. My thoughts of a happy meeting were destroyed and I tried my best to hide my emotions. I was devastated. I was fighting so hard to hold back the tears.

I said, "Well, just tell me."

He answered, "She doesn't want to dance with you anymore."

I said, "Why the hell not? We were getting along just fine and we had our choreography done and were ready for the show!"

Finally, all the pieces in my mind were coming together, her trying and wanting to take over the choreography and the director contacting me to let her do some choreography made sense. To top it all off we hadn't signed a contract so it was easy for them to get rid of me. In Canada, if the director was interested in working with you, a contract was signed before your first day of work. It wasn't the case here in Greece and there was nothing I could do about it. I had no agent, no manager, no representative, and no nothing.

I turned to him and said, "Why don't you get rid of her?"

He responded, "I know Taso she is unreasonable and a bit of a diva, she was over the top, but unfortunately the show is for the stars."

I knew he was right; I just didn't want to accept it.

He then said, "Your professionalism has been amazing. We all love you and enjoyed working with you and really wanted to work with you, this is very, very hard for me to do this."

I saw the disappointment in his face, it didn't look like it was an act and his feelings were genuine. I was trying so hard to keep my composure, it was like a war was going on inside to keep me from showing my feelings.

I said to him, "I want to be on Season Four."

He said, "Yes."

Then I turned and said, "This is fricken bullshit and I can't believe that the star has the upper hand and not the directors."

He then proceeded to explain in English and I snapped at him and told him to speak Greek to me. He said, "I understand, you have every right to be upset."

I was sitting in a chair across from his desk trying to take all this in as best as I could. I couldn't look him straight in the face as he was talking to me, not because I was angry with him, I wasn't, I was just so hurt and upset with the situation. I was looking out an open window at a big beautiful green tree, just full of life swaying and dancing in the light wind trying to contain my emotions. I felt like the whole world around me came crashing down and my dreams were being, crushed, stomped and handed back to me in an envelope.

It felt like the most devastating part of my life. I couldn't handle it anymore, I just had to let some tears flow down my face as I was looking out the window.

I turned to the director and said, "I can't believe I am 33 years old and I am sitting in your office crying. I am so embarrassed." And I told him about the seven Greek communities back in Canada, which was about 10,000 people who were waiting to see me, "How am I going to face these people?"

He responded, "I am 39 years old and I want to cry too. Just tell people that it didn't work out."

I just looked at him with a blank stare. I could see in his body language that he was upset too. I then proceeded to give him a Canadian flag keychain. He took it and said, "Thank you very much, now I will definitely not forget you."

Then I saw he had a Kenny stuffed doll on the windowsill from **South Park**. I took it and put a Canadian flag pin on it and said, "Do you remember the song **Blame Canada**?"

He said, "Yes," and we laughed.

I got up from my chair and said thank you very much as I proceeded to walk to the door. I shook his hand and again said thank you very much for all your efforts, hard work and to everybody at the TV station and production company for being so very nice to me.

He said, "You're welcome and I am very, very sorry. I know how much you wanted to be on the show." He then proceeded to tell me to go to Alexia's office and she will take care of the rest. I could tell he was upset and didn't want to take me there so I went by myself. He quickly turned away and went into his office, closing the door behind him.

I walked to Alexia's office to hand in my receipts for my airfare. She was in tears and gave me a hug. I said thank you for all of your hard work. I put on my sunglasses with tears streaming down my face, turned away and said goodbye.

I left the building with a heavy heart of pain and disappointment. I wasn't expecting to hear this news. I hung my head and walked in utter pain. I was so upset. I couldn't gather my thoughts to think properly of what my next move would be. I still had some tears running down my face. I stopped and had a thought; at least I have a good story to write in my book one day. I turned this negative experience into a positive one and it put a smile on my face.

As disappointed and unhappy as I was feeling, I always had a thought that I wanted to write a book one day about my journey of giving my best and giving it my all to fulfill my dreams. I always wanted to share my experiences with the world. I arrived at the bus stop and got on the bus with my head held higher than it was a little while earlier. I did have a tear or two coming down my face, but I was feeling much better as I wiped them off my face and got on the bus.

I was sitting on a packed bus and was starting to feel much better. I looked out the window as the bus went by the many buildings on Kiffissias Avenue. I finally got to my stop and made my way to my hotel. I was dreading telling my friends from all over the world, from Greece to Canada. It's not like I didn't want to tell them, I just didn't want to give them bad news. I knew it was going to be a long- winded story I would have to tell over and over again and again.

I got to my hotel room and the first thing I did was post a Facebook message informing everybody of what happened. I then turned off my computer, picked up my phone and started calling my friends here in Greece. They all had the same reaction. They swore her up and down calling her every name imaginable, showing they were very upset for me.

In the early evening a group of friends drove down to the hotel, picked me up and we went out for a coffee. I told them the details from start to finish of what happened earlier today. By the time I was finished, to tell you the truth I was fine and felt much better.

My friend Foti said, "Tasos, she pulled a publicity stunt." In other words, the star gets the media coverage whether it's positive or negative. It gets them in the spotlight and that's what they want, not all stars, but some will do just about anything. Now it all made more sense to me and I was over it by the evening. I wasn't so upset with the star either; I guess I was more upset with the situation. I had worked so hard to get to this point in my career and it was all gone in a flash. A good cry is good because after a good cry you feel much more relieved and a hell of a lot better. What doesn't kill you makes you stronger and I wasn't going to give it all up, like I said, I worked very, very hard to get to this point.

After I had my long extended coffee break with my friends I asked them to drop me off at the studio where I was supposed to practice the professional routine with the other dancers for the opening number of the show. I arrived outside of the studio and my heart was pounding with fear at how I was going to be looked at or treated by the other professional dancers. As I made my way up the stairs my heart pounded more and more with fear with every step I took. I finally got to the top and opened the door to the studio. I greeted everybody and said I had an announcement to make. Everybody gathered around me in a semi-circle and were attentive to hear what I was going to say. I announced that I was leaving the show because the star wanted another dance partner. They all rolled their eyes and said, "Don't worry we know it's not your fault, stars love to do this kind of stuff and they sometimes don't care who it hurts. It's all about them." I was so happy that they understood and smiled instantly. What a relief.

I opened my gym bag, pulled out a small plastic bag and gave all of them a Canadian flag pin. They smiled and said, "Thank you."

Some pinned their pins on their purses others on their bags and some on their shirts. One dancer turned to me and said, "Taso don't worry, the same thing happened to me in Season One." Another dancer stood up and said, "I admire the fact that you came and told us, I wouldn't have been able to do that".

Another dancer said, "Taso, we really learned a lot from you telling us. You are brave and don't be embarrassed."

I was so touched and happy with everybody's reaction, it was truly unbelievable. I didn't know what to expect when I walked into the studio. Another dancer, Eftychia Marketaki, who is an amazing dancer with an incredible style and flare said, "Taso we love you too and don't forget that we are also upset at this situation." She must have read some comments that friends had posted on my Facebook page earlier in the day. I hadn't seen anything yet because I hadn't checked my messages since I wrote the message on my wall. I was so touched with happiness and gave her a hug.

Then I saw the new guy who was taking my spot. I was so happy and couldn't have been happier that he was taking over. On the actual day of the audition, I was chatting with this same guy for about an hour because the schedule was behind and he was next in line after myself. He was truly a whole-hearted and kind individual. I wished him good luck and I hoped he'd do well on the show. He shook my hand with delight. It was time for them to start dancing, so I stayed and watched the dancers practice their opening routine.

After they finished one of the dancers took me back to the hotel. It was an emotional day and I was tired, but before I went to sleep, I turned on my laptop and checked my Facebook messages. It was full of positive responses from friends and family from back home in Canada and all over the world. They were all supportive and told me not to worry and to keep going. I turned off my computer and went to sleep.

THE GREEK MEDIA

NOVEMBER 6, 2012

After a good sleep I woke up and decided to stay in bed and lounge around the hotel room for the day. I had nothing planned and I thought a nice break after all of this havoc was well deserved. I turned on my laptop, checked my email and Facebook accounts. On my Facebook page there was a new friend request from a Greek TV station, "Star Channel".

This channel is the gossip station and I wondered, what should I do? I didn't accept their request. I know responding to a gossip show wasn't the right answer. I didn't want to create problems for anybody. I know this station had a job to do, but I didn't want to be a part of it all anymore. I just wanted to go home. A friend in Greece sent me a message on Facebook telling me to see this video clip that was from the "Star Channel." My pictures were downloaded from my Facebook account and put on this gossip show. It was a panel of five people that brought the gossip of showbiz to the public in Greece. The clip was about my celebrity that wanted a new dance partner and how another celebrity was now doing the same thing on the show too. While the panel was discussing what was going on, there was a screen behind them with a few pictures of me dancing in past professional competitions. It was kind of cool. They had nothing negative to say about me, but they did about the stars who wanted new partners and they did get the new partners they requested. The panel stated how spoiled some stars can be and how inconsiderate they are and act like divas. The panel was appalled that the stars have so much power to do what they want on a show. Gossip magazines and shows in Greece can be very descriptive and explicit and say just about anything they like; whereas gossip in North America is not as harsh.

I was also getting friend requests on Facebook from a few other panel members. They wanted to interview me and were asking what happened on the show. I didn't know what to do so I called my friends and cousins to get some opinions. I also called the production company of *Dancing with the Stars*. They all told me the same thing; not to speak to any gossip television stations or magazines in Greece because that will destroy my chances of ever working again in Greece. I didn't want to do that because if another opportunity came around I wanted it to be given to me, not taken away from me. All I wanted was some guidance.

I thought the production company was protecting their own interests, but everybody else was telling me the same thing. Plus, the woman from the production company was honest and genuine with me too.

I decided not to get interviewed and knew I was doing the right thing. Sometimes the hardest part in this business is the people who are protecting their own interests and when you are new, like me, you don't know what to do. I often go with a gut feeling, we all do, and we all know that going with your gut feeling is the best thing to do. It's the universe, God or something sending you a message advising you to do the right thing.

I spent the rest of the day online looking for auditions in North America. I came across an audition in Hollywood, Florida for the Royal Caribbean Cruise line. They were looking for singers for the Broadway shows they have on their luxurious ships. The audition was for December 2nd. I made a quick decision. I said to myself, I must go to this audition. I must keep going.

If I have learned anything in this business thus far, it's full of rejection, you have to be strong, have a good cry, pick yourself up off the floor, dust yourself off and keep going. All these experiences just made me stronger and I was becoming stronger and stronger. I booked my flight from Toronto to Florida. Good God I love credit cards.

I was leaving Greece on November 5th only to leave home again in about two weeks for Florida. I just had to keep moving forward. I called my friends in Greece and in Canada and told them what I was going to do next. Everybody was happy for me and admired my perseverance. I was and will always be grateful of the support from everyone. I had some more great dinners, coffee breaks and outings while I was in Greece. I spent my last ten days visiting relatives and my grandfather who lived just outside of Tripoli, a city about a two-hour bus ride south of Athens in the Peloponnese.

BACK HOME TO CANADA

NOVEMBER 20, 2012

I got up early in the morning, picked up my suitcase, checked out of the hotel, called a taxi and made my way to the Athens International Airport. My flight was at 9am. I checked in at the counter, went through customs and got on my nine-hour flight home with a transfer through Rome, Italy. The flight was smooth and I arrived in Toronto early in the evening.

I turned on my cell phone as soon as I walked off the plane to inform my parents that I arrived home safely. I collected my suitcase and went through customs. Got into a taxi and headed for Hamilton. Home sweet home. Even though I was happy to be home, I was a little sad at the same time to be home so early, it was kind of bittersweet.

In the taxi, I was dreading having to tell the story over and over again for a second time. I had to tell people why I was home; this time it was more than my family and friends. It was the Greek community and because I am so active in the community I knew I was going to be asked again and again from so many people about what happened. Good God, next time something like this happens I should send out a press release. Nevertheless, it had to be done; there was no way around it.

I resumed work at the family restaurant and the dance studio because I was really low on money, well, the fact was I just didn't have any money left, so I was desperate. I started my singing, dancing, and aerial silks classes. I needed to make fast money because I was going to Hollywood, Florida at the end of the month to audition for the Royal Caribbean Cruise Line. I didn't have any time to waste and I needed to prepare and review my singing material for the audition. I was doing all this to prepare for my next audition and I did find some time during the day to keep searching for auditions. I had gone to many auditions at this point, even before I went to Greece, but I was always searching online for auditions of all types, all the time. It is just the nature of being in this line of work. It was nearing the end of the month and I was ready to go to my audition in Florida.

FLORIDA

DECEMBER 1, 2012

I woke up at 6am, got showered and dressed and took a taxi to Toronto Pearson International Airport. On the way, I was thinking what it would be like to be on a ship singing and dancing. I was daydreaming of different ports all over the world, meeting different people and seeing different places. I pictured myself where I wanted to be, hoping something in God's universe would get me to being on stage or in a film making a living of what I loved to do. I finally arrived at the airport and went through the usual drill of checking in and the rest of the fun stuff at customs and got on my three-hour flight for Fort Lauderdale, Florida.

I arrived in Florida to warm weather, picked up my rental car and made my way to my hotel. I have been to Fort Lauderdale, Florida with a group of good friends a few times before and knew my way around major streets and highways in southern Florida.

It was fantastic to be in a familiar place because I didn't have to run around trying to figure out where to go and how to get there. Southern Florida is not very hard to navigate; it just has the I-95 and it's Turnpike, making for easy travel. The next plus was that Hollywood and Fort Lauderdale were about a 15-minute drive via the highway. I arrived at my hotel, checked in, showered and got in my car to find the audition location.

Royal Caribbean has its own studios in Hollywood where the talent goes for auditions and where they practice for the shows onboard their ships. I found the studios and made my way back to my hotel. I relaxed for the evening and went to sleep early because of my early morning audition. Florida is in the same time zone as Toronto so I didn't have to get over jetlag.

The following day I woke up at 7:30am, got ready and drove 15 minutes to the Royal Caribbean Productions. It was about 8:30am when I arrived. I think it's always important to arrive an hour early for auditions, better early than late. I always bring a book or crossword puzzle to relax. I hadn't eaten breakfast, so I walked down to the breakfast house about a block from the studios. After breakfast I still had about 45 minutes to kill, so I walked around the block a few times mentally preparing myself for my audition and singing my audition songs. Okay, so I am a weirdo, I was walking around the block singing songs! It was a bright sunny day, what else could you ask for? Sure I was passing people on the street and they were looking at me funny, but who cares, they got a second or two of entertainment as they walked by me.

Finally, I made my way to the front doors of the building at about 9:45am. I walked in and there were about 50 people also waiting to audition as singers and dancers. I registered as a singer. I never would go to auditions that were primarily for dancing unless they were ballroom auditions. I didn't have the criteria they were asking for, in other words, I couldn't do the pirouettes, leaps and jumps. I have some training in ballet and jazz, but I was a chicken and wouldn't go for dancing auditions. I will drive up the courage one day and go to one. Now was not the time.

I made my way to a colourful waiting area that looked like I was on a ship. I took a seat and started chatting with people around me. Most of the people came from various parts of Florida, others came from South Carolina, Nebraska and California. I was the one who travelled the farthest. They were stunned when I told them I came from Canada. You see, singing auditions only last for maybe five minutes. You are asked to bring two contrasting songs, a slow song and an up tempo song. You are only asked to sing 16 to 32 bars of music, each page having 16 bars of music, in other words, two pages of music and each song usually lasts for about one minute. At some auditions the people in charge tell you only to sing 16 bars of music, of one or both songs. This is usual if there are about 100 people or more auditioning and it all depends on the director too. It's all over so quickly and this is why my fellow "auditioners" were stunned that I came from so far away.

At about 9:58am a really, cheerful African American man dressed in every colour in the rainbow greeted us. He kindly directed the singers to one studio and the dancers to another. We were given a number when we registered, I was number 95, like I said, there were over 50 people at the audition and they just gave us a random number that was put on a list next to our names. I was waiting outside of the designated studio and was starting to get a little nervous. As I see it, being a little nervous is good because it just keeps you on your toes, attentive and grounded.

I heard my number called. I was ready and walking in I said to myself, "Give it your best shot." I greeted the two people in charge and they greeted me back with a friendly hello and a warm smile. The directing staff want you to succeed, they aren't out to get you, this is what I heard from directors in the past, so they don't create an intimidating atmosphere. I handed my music to the pianist and greeted and introduced myself to the camera. Some auditions are recorded because the director may go back and review what was done to reconsider his choice.

I asked the pianist to start playing, so he did. I wasn't ready to start singing. In all the other auditions that I have been to when you ask the pianist to start playing, they always start by saying, "Five, six, seven, eight … or, one, two, three …" and then they start playing. He went immediately into the song.

I missed the first few notes because I was waiting for the cue. I was thrown off guard. It was a horrible start to an audition. I asked the pianist to stop and start again. I was disappointed inside; though, I didn't show it and I kept my composure. My heart was racing like I was about to fall over from all the anxiety that immediately built up inside my body. Yet, I maintained a smile on the outside.

I finished my song and wasn't asked to sing my second song. The director said thanks which means no thanks, we don't want you. The fact that I didn't get to sing my second song, in such a small audition, means they weren't interested at all.

I failed to mention earlier that out of the 50 people, about ten were singers, so it was a very small audition. It was game over for me once again. I planned to stay for a week in hopes that I was going to get the job and be spending time doing paper work with the company and all else that would have needed to get done. Now I had a week to do a whole lot of nothing. Well, I mean, I was in south Florida and there was plenty to do here. I spent the whole week socializing at tourist bars, making friends and going to South Beach in Miami.

I did have some ideas on how to try and get work with one of the cruise companies, or make myself known to them at the very least. It's always an adventure in my world. On December 3rd I went back to the Royal Caribbean Productions Studios and I asked to speak with the singing director who was in charge. The lovely receptionist, who called him at his desk, told me that he was busy and couldn't come to see me at that very moment and that he may be free soon. I asked if I could wait and was allowed to wait. I sat in a nice white chair and started reading a cooking magazine; it was the only thing on the coffee table in front of me. Well, at least I was learning something about cooking. I looked at my watch and ten minutes went by and then 20 minutes and then 30 minutes and then almost 40 minutes went by. I finally realized that he wasn't coming out to see me. The nice receptionist told me to leave my email address and he would communicate via email. I did and left.

I had another idea. On December 4th I decided to go and hand in a resume into Carnival Cruise Line, but their head office was in Miami, a 45-minute drive from Fort Lauderdale. I had all the time in the world, so I went.

I arrived at their headquarters and went through security in the parking lot. I was greeted and asked, "What are you here for?"

I replied, "I am here to hand in a resume to work as an entertainer."

He replied, "They only take resumes electronically." And proceeded to hand me a sheet with the email address on it. I looked at it disappointed that I couldn't speak to somebody. It has come to the point in our fast paced world that you can't even talk to a person for a brief moment when you want to hand in a resume.

I looked at him and said, "I am here from Canada for various auditions and can you please let me go through?" I was practically begging. Well I wasn't practically begging, I was begging.

He said, "Fine, go through." I was probably driving him nuts begging and pleading, so he finally broke and I succeeded.

I parked my car and went into the main tower and there was an African American security guard in her mid-30s. I approached her desk with a smile and my resume in my hands.

I said, "Hello." She greeted me with a warm smile and said a hello back. I said, "I have a resume that I wanted to hand in to the person in charge for entertainment."

She asked, "How did you get through parking security?"

I replied, "I begged!" She laughed and smiled at me. Well, I was starting to flirt with her at this point and she was smiling back and she was getting all giddy. I thought to myself, she was going to let me in to see whomever was in charge. She then handed me the same piece of paper that the parking lot security guard gave me — the one with the email address on it to send my resume.

I smiled at her, laughed and begged at the same time to hand it in personally. She informed me, "This is the only way, its policy and it has been like this for a number of years." And then she smiled at me and said, "Baby I am sorry."

I then replied in a funny fashion, "If I throw myself on the floor and start crying like a child would you let me go through?" By this time I knew I wasn't going to get in no matter what I would try to say or do, so we were both laughing and having fun with the situation.

She said, "Baby I am really sorry."

I stopped laughing and said, "Thank you for your efforts have a nice day." I left having tried all my tactics; I tried everything I could possibly think of without being too annoying and pushy. I went to my car and said at least I tried to myself. I got into the car and headed back to Fort Lauderdale.

DECEMBER 5, 2012

I woke up at 10:30am, turned on my laptop to check my emails to see if I had some type of response from any Royal Caribbean singing director. There wasn't an email. Then I waited about an hour or so to check my email account again, but nothing. I finally called the production office and they said I will get a response via email. I figured I had to stop what I was doing, no one was responding. Then, I had another bright idea. I am always full of ideas. I have to try it at least once, twice and thrice. Okay, sometimes I tried more than three times four or five; at that point I just altered my approach. I've got to get creative. I am an artist that is what we are known for: our creativity.

I called Carnival Cruise Line and asked to speak with somebody who was in charge of the entertainment to see if I could make an appointment to come and hand in a resume. Once again the answer was, "No, it's only done electronically."

I said, "Thanks and have a nice day." I was all out of ideas and there was nothing I could do without getting into trouble looking like I was a crazy Greek Canadian trying to make my dream a reality. I could only go to the head offices and call so many times. There was nothing else I could do at this moment. I just got out of bed, got dressed and went to the Fort Lauderdale beach and enjoyed my day well into the evening.

DECEMBER 6, 2012

The past few times I had been in Florida I had gone to a ballroom and Latin dance studio where I participated in group classes and their open dancing classes on Thursday and Friday nights. On one trip I met Patti, this really nice lady in her early 50s and we became friends. After that I would call her up when I was in town and we would meet up for lunch or dinner and then go dancing. I called her and told her about my escapades of trying to find work and updated her on my life.

Like usual, we went dancing, she told me about a gentleman by the name of John who had a dance company. His company took people (who dance ballroom and Latin dancing socially) on a cruise and he needed dance hosts. It was called *Dancing at Sea*.

He would bring about 40 people on a major cruise line and hire a few dance teachers to give lessons about four to five times while on the one-week cruise. As a dance host, you would participate on these cruises and just dance. I would dance with all the women when there was open dancing and I would participate in the group dance classes too. All expenses were paid for as compensation: it would be a free trip. I thought to myself what a fabulous idea and I was interested.

I met John at the dance hall and he was delighted to meet me. He was observing my friend and me as we danced and complimented my dancing ability. He asked me to come on board his next cruise! We exchanged contact information and said he would be in contact with me. So, I made some type of contact after all. It made me feel much better and I felt I had accomplished something. I enjoyed the rest of the evening dancing and socializing.

DECEMBER 7, 2012

Today was my last day in Florida and I thought I would give it one more chance to contact the singing director or scout at the Royal Caribbean office. I still hadn't received an email. I got in my car and drove to the office again. I thought one more chance wouldn't hurt. Once again I was greeted by the friendly receptionist and I asked if I could speak with him, she called his desk and he replied that he was busy and couldn't speak with me and he would reply through email. I said thanks and just left. I was disappointed that he couldn't have the common courtesy to give some type of response, I mean how busy could you possibly be at a job. I work like the rest of the world and I return messages left by people, even if it's an inquiry. I still see the value and importance in that. People are calling you and your company because they are interested in working for you, does that not hold any merit? After I got home to Canada I checked my email daily for a few weeks searching for a reply and he never did respond. I couldn't believe it. I was just so disappointed that I couldn't even get a simple email, something that takes just a few minutes to write and send at the click of a button.

I left Fort Lauderdale and went from sunny hot skies to cold weather in Canada. I resumed all my usual work while thinking of what to do next. My wheels were always turning and figuring out ways to move forward. I needed to have a mental break before I went crazy, but I did have a new great idea: I was going to start flamenco dancing! I figured I would have a fun time with good friends and cousins and enjoy the Christmas season. Okay, so I did calm down for a little bit. I was just so determined.

JANUARY 2013

The Christmas and New Year season was wonderful. I spent it as usual with my family, friends and a lot of good food. I had been enjoying my flamenco lessons for about a month now. The teacher was fantastic. I loved it so much, but I had to stop. It was getting to be too expensive. It cost $65 an hour for a private lesson, which is pretty standard for any style of dance for private lessons. The problem was, the studio was in downtown Toronto and I had to pay for parking, which was $20, so in total, with parking it cost $85. I couldn't simply afford it with everything else I had going on. All my other ballroom training and silks training were in Toronto, but they weren't downtown and I didn't have the expense of paying for parking when every penny counts. I wanted to add more skills to my repertoire of talents so I started searching for something else.

I had taken some ballet classes in the past and I had a good understanding of style and movement and I wanted to do more. Adult ballet classes were hard to find in the greater Toronto area, so I searched online and found a Facebook page for adult ballet classes here in Hamilton. I called and was greeted by a heavy accented Russian woman telling me times and prices. Group classes were about $16 per person and that was affordable. It was in Hamilton, so I didn't have to drive very far and parking was free after 6pm, which made life much easier.

I started going three evenings a week, boy was it killer hard, and it was much harder than other ballet classes that I had taken in the past. We had a fantastic teacher from Russia. Her name was Irina, she was in her 50s, had a sexy dancer's body, fiery red hair and was very strict in her teaching style. She made sure we had proper posture at all times and proper movement; working hard was her game. She was very comical too. She always made jokes and was laughing all the time. She was just a delight to work with; she was the style of teacher I wanted. I had been looking for a teacher like her for a long time. She was never rude, insulting or demeaning. I loved this woman and later on, when I got comfortable, I called her the dragon lady. She had a very high expectation of how ballet should be executed, but never, never put any of her students down.

This artistic woman who danced for the St. Petersburg Ballet for 20 years and possessed a PhD in dance was amazing. I wish the industry could learn from her because people in this business can be disrespectful, rude and demeaning at times — which I find completely unnecessary. She got along with everybody with her great work ethic. She gave us all nicknames in class that best described our personalities, or who she thought we looked like. She called this one girl "Celine Dion", another "Tinker Bell" and the list goes on and on. Out of a class of about 20, there was only about two to three other guys in the class. One guy she called "Iron Man" and she had a list of names for me, "Zeus" because I was Greek, "Pavarotti" because I could sing, "Peter Pan" because I came into class one day with my beard shaved off my face and I looked like I was ten years old. I just enjoyed the class. I was getting into shape and fast because of her tactics.

I also thought it would be a good idea to take some acting classes. I hadn't taken them in years. As I see it, there is always something to learn and a refresher in life from time to time is good, because we learn new material and refine old material.

I took acting classes every Saturday morning at a local theatre company in Hamilton. It was simply great. I was learning more about acting through various group and individual activities. There were people of all ages in the classes from 16 years old to people in their 50s. Acting classes not only teach you how to act, but also give you confidence through various activities to speak in front of large groups of people. For example, learning a monologue from a play. This is spoken independently in front of a group of people and it gives you the confidence you need to speak using plenty of feeling and emotion. I enjoyed them very much and I learned plenty of new material that I will use in the future.

At the beginning of January I got a phone call from John, the gentleman that I met in Florida who was in charge of the dance cruises. He asked me if I was free the first week of February to come on a cruise as a dance host. I immediately said yes. I did have a million things to do as usual, but I would figure out a way to get on this cruise. I managed to get all my dance classes covered and all else that I had to do, I just delayed everything for the week, which was fine as usual.

He organized the trip with the Royal Caribbean Cruise Line and the ship was named the *Independence of the Seas*. I had never been on a cruise ship before in my life and was very excited. The seven-day cruise departed from Fort Lauderdale, Florida and it was going to Saint Kitts, Saint Maarten, Puerto Rico and Haiti.

FEBRUARY 2013

I flew down to Florida and arrived at the docks at about 11am. The *Independence of the Seas* was one of the largest ships in the world.

As I approached the vessel I was amazed at the size of this massive piece of iron and steel floating on the water. It was like a city skyscraper that would move with ease. It was like five downtown city blocks long, at least that is what it looked like. I kept looking at this ship and wondered how such a thing could float on water? It was mesmerizing.

I boarded and was greeted by the friendly staff and a photographer that took pictures if you wanted it, touristy stuff. I opted out of the picture and walked around the ship in awe. I wanted to see as much as I could before we embarked on the sea. The ship was so beautifully decorated, shiny and pristine. I had never been to the Caribbean before and always heard it was a great place to visit. I went to the upper deck of the ship and it was full of people waiting to depart. Everyone was on deck and looking out to the land. The captain sounded the horn and we started to move. I just couldn't get over the fact that such a huge thing was floating on the water and now moving. It was cool.

About an hour or so after leaving the docks we had a meet and greet with the group of people that were participating in the ballroom and Latin cruise. We had a brief orientation of what we were going to do for the next week, from dance classes, dancing in the evening and to the various land excursions that were available on the islands. The group was mostly in their 50s and 60s; they were retired and enjoying cruises. They were all super friendly, ready to learn new dance moves and use their new dance moves for the evenings of dancing.

These people all had previous dance experience and came to progress more in their skills. They made me feel extremely welcomed. Typically, dance host jobs are given to older more distinguished men well into their 40s and 50s. I was in my early 30s, so it was nice to be with these people. I enjoyed laughing with them at dinner-time, socializing by the pool during the day, going on excursions and just plain chatting about life. It was wonderful and I made some new friends.

I gravitated to these people because they had many different talents. We had a lot in common; they liked to participate in different activities like myself. It was nice to see people double my age balance a family and fulfill their life dreams. It was amazing because they were successful, very successful. I've been given a hard time by many people back home for the simple reason that they thought I was doing too many things in life and that I would never be able to manage it all. Well, when I came home, boy did I tell everybody I met a group of people like myself who had families too, something that I also wanted at some point in life. I met one gentleman, Roger, who was a fashion designer. He had a business degree and he completed his PhD at 54, and was doing very well for himself. I also met Sylvia who was a gospel singer.

She travelled to all 50 states during her career, raising and home schooling her well-rounded children. These were just a few, but it was nice to see they created the lives they chose to live. Now I have proof that it can be done. These types of lifestyles are not for everybody, but it sure was for me. I just loved it!

HARD AT WORK

FEBRUARY, MARCH, APRIL, MAY 2013

The next four months were spent doing what I have been doing up until this point: singing classes, acting classes, ballet classes, ballroom and Latin dance training, going to the gym and still struggling with the aerial silks (not going to give up). I have also been going to audition after audition, day in and day out rearranging work schedules to make auditions on time. I just want to be on stage and in film. I turned 34 on March 10th and had a fantastic birthday celebration with family and friends.

I was working harder and harder. I was perfecting and refining my talents, minute by minute, day by day and just using all the time I had. I needed to get more creative and find a way to make myself known. So, I had this bright idea. I just watched **My Big Fat Greek Wedding** again for the fourth time. I loved it, it's funny and hey it's Greek too.

I wanted to get in contact with Nia Vardalos. She is Greek-Canadian, and in my mind that's the perfect combination! My challenge was, how on God's green earth was I going to do this? I knew she was from Winnipeg, which was a few hours flight away from where I lived, but then I thought to myself what the hell am I going to do there?

My next bright idea was to fly to Winnipeg, stay there for a month and go to the Greek church every Sunday and hope to run into Nia's parents and give them my resume, so they could give it to her. But the fact was, I just didn't have the money to stay in Winnipeg for more than a day never mind a month. So I had to scrap that idea, or well just let it linger at the back of my mind.

I knew through the "Greek grapevine" that the late Father Demetrios Karambelas (who was a fantastic man) from the Greek Orthodox church in Hamilton (where I attended) was transferred to the Greek church in Winnipeg. He presided over her wedding ceremony many years earlier. The late Father's children, which were in there late 40s now, George, Ted and Chrysa went to the same Greek church that I went to in Hamilton and have always been helpful and supportive when I have a bright idea.

So I had another bright idea. I was going to ask if they knew how I could get in touch with Nia Vardalos. I asked them, but they didn't know and were sorry they couldn't be of any help. I said thank you very much and just kept thinking how am I going to get her my resume. I told a bunch of friends at the Greek community and they thought that my idea of getting her my resume was fantastic. All I kept thinking in my head was how the hell was I going to do this without looking like some sort of weirdo? I said to myself, there has to be a way.

Now it's spring and Easter is near, or *Pascha* as we call it in Greek. I was preparing for a lot of food and good Greek fun. The night before Palm Sunday I worked at our family restaurant until 3am serving the happy crowd from the bars, as I have been for about ten years on weekends. I was serving many of the finest, happiest people, in other words, really drunk people and by the time we would clean up and get home it was generally about 4am. My mother reminded me to go to church the night before because she and my father were going to be working on Sunday and I was to go and get palms for our family. It's a tradition and I have been going every year since I was a child.

As I was opening my eyes at 11am on Sunday morning, I stared at the ceiling and felt like my eyes were going to pop out of my head because I was still so tired. I decided I could sleep for another ten minutes and then catch the last 20 minutes of the service, get the palms and make my Greek mother happy. I was only a ten-minute drive from the church and our Greek church services end about noon. I knew because it was a special day and there would usually be an extra prayer at the end of the service so it would finish about 12:15pm, so I knew I was safe. My 20 minutes of sleep went until 12:15pm and by this time the service was over. I opted to stay in bed, turn on my computer and check my email and Facebook accounts. I saw a message sent at 12:12pm.

My friend John sent me a message to say that Nia Vardalos' parents were at church in Hamilton. Shocked and surprised I flew out of bed and immediately called him. He told me to get here as quick as I could to give my resume to them. I was looking in my bedroom mirror while speaking with him, I started to laugh and so did he, he didn't know why he was laughing, but I did. I was laughing at myself because I had huge red pillow creases that covered more than half my face. I told him and he laughed too.

I said, "I can't go out in public looking like this, especially to the Greek community where I know everybody. They would know I just rolled out of bed and showed up for the after church coffee hour!" I thanked him for thinking of me and said goodbye. My crazy laughter turned into disappointment. I went back to bed, stared at the ceiling and thought I am being punished for not going to church. I had a great chance and missed it all because I didn't get out of bed at 11am. Oh well, I didn't dwell on it too long.

Later that afternoon I called John back and asked, "Why on God's green earth were the Vardalos' here in Hamilton? They live in Winnipeg."

He replied, "I think they have a daughter or relative that lives in Toronto and they were going to spend *Pascha* with them. I guess it has something to do with their connection with the late Father Demetrios."

I said, "I see, that makes sense then." I told him I was still disappointed that I couldn't meet them.

He replied, "It just wasn't the right time."

I guess back to the thinking board. I had to continue working, that's all I could do at this point in time and continue going to auditions. It was now the end of May and I was chatting with Sharon, a gal in my ballet class. I was telling her how hard I was working at trying to make my dream come true. She was doing the same thing; she was an actor too. She was working hard at chasing her dream.

Sharon suggested that I start doing background work, which means I would be making some money doing what I enjoyed. I came home after ballet class, searched online and found a few background agencies. In this wonderful business of show business you are allowed to have multiple background agents and one principal agent. Those are the rules. I sent them my resume and within one week I had three background agents offer me representation, but I opted to just have one background agent. I thought it would be easier to keep track of work from one agent because I already had a busy schedule.

I started doing background work immediately and from there on, I was doing it on a weekly basis. It was a step in the right direction. It was one step closer to my dream. It was the coolest thing to be on movie and TV sets, because I had never done that before in my life.

The days were long and could get extremely boring. Most of the time we were in a holding area. This area was always separate from the actual set. The days were at least ten to twelve hours long and could start as early as 7am. Most of the time was spent just waiting and waiting. Sometimes we were used for a total of two to three hours and the rest of the time was spent in holding. We were paid the entire duration of the time and were fed well, which was a good thing. The food on the sets was great; long buffets with so much variety.

Sharon suggested I bring something to occupy my time, so now I always bring a pen and note pad, just in case I meet new people or make contacts in the industry. I would bring crossword puzzles, magazines and books to read. I often started chatting up a storm with people because I love to talk with people. I slowly was discovering that most of the background people were struggling in the industry just like I was. I thought, I didn't want to struggle, but I guess that it is just the nature of it until you get a principal role of some sort. I was always trying to find ways to get my name out into the acting world and for now this would do.

SUMMER 2013

JUNE 2013

The summer was well on its way and the weather was warm and sunny, it was a fantastic start to the season. I decided to register for a summer intensive theatre arts program that ran in July at a local theatre company. The course was just over four weeks long with classes that included acting, improv, singing, dancing and finished off with a Broadway production. Two weeks were spent doing classes and the other two weeks were spent doing the production. It was intense.

Working on a production in just over two weeks is killer work. I decided to send off my registration form and prepare for this program. I was also participating in another local community theatre show as well. I had a full plate between work, the first theatre company and doing this program. It was going to be a lot of work for the summer, but I was willing to work hard to get all the training I could possible get.

JULY 2013

The classes started just after Canada Day long weekend. They ran five days a week from 9am to 3pm for the next month. When I was filling out the registration form for the theatre program there was a line that said the program was open for registration for people 15 years of age and up; I thought people of all ages attending the program was great.

I arrived to the first day of classes and was greeted by a bunch of happy, bubbly teenagers. As 9am approached I realized there wasn't anyone else my age — not even close to my age. I was wondering if I was in the right program and I discovered I was, because the other programs being run were for children.

I started chatting with the "young ins" and slowly found out that I was the oldest of all of them, by about 14 to 17 years. It was going to be an interesting experience. I didn't mind working with these adolescents because they were here to learn and so was I. I was just expecting to see more of a mixed crowd. There were about 30 students in the class and we were split up into three groups of about ten. Classes were on a rotational basis, singing, dancing, acting and improv.

We attended these classes at various points throughout the day. We all had dance class at 9am and then we went to various other classes throughout the day. It was nice being with these young minds, I felt like a teenager again. They worked hard and were very animated. They have these dreams of making it in the world, without knowing how hard it can actually get as they mature with age. They were full of life, they were full of happiness, and they were full of innocence. It was nice to be with them. They reminded me of myself when I was their age; finding myself and finding out where I wanted to go in life. I learned so much from these young talented minds. In life, we learn from people of all ages, young and old. I appreciated every moment I spent with them. The director, Lou, was animated too and could freak out at the drop of a hat; he was great and we all learned lots from him too.

It was now mid-July and our insightful classes were finished. I was really tired from being there all day, going to work in the evenings and being part of another theatre company. My days were 12 to 14 hours long and I knew it would become more intense in the next few weeks because I had to learn music and dancing too — just to add to all of my fun.

Our days were intense for the next two and a half weeks. Everybody was stressed out because a show was going to be put on and we were pressed for time. Costumes needed to be made, the right notes needed to be sung, the right dance moves needed to happen, the right lines needed to be learned, a set needed to be built, the orchestra needed to learn their music, the lighting had to be adjusted and the microphones ... the list went on and on. It was a lot of work. Everybody was on their toes because our director and singing director were stressed out because they wanted the show done right. They could lose it at any point in time. Everybody was stressed. The big guys wanted us to do well and we wanted to do well. It was hard. I was falling apart inside because I was overwhelmed with everything. I just wanted to work as hard as possible so I could make my dreams come true. I just kept pushing myself to move forward. I knew I was just refining and learning all of my singing, dancing and acting skills. It was worth it.

AUGUST 2013

Our show, *A Chorus Line*, went on the first week of August and I played the role of Don Kerr. The last two weekends of the month I was part of the chorus in *The Pyjama Game* with the other theatre company. I loved being on stage. It was uplifting. I felt alive. I was full of excitement and my heart pounded with delight. We had standing ovations every night. I would lose myself in the roaring of the crowd and I was happy to take part with other people in making the audience feel wonderful after our shows. We received compliments and flowers as well. We had cast parties afterwards with lots of laughter and tears of joy. Our directors were proud of our hard work and were moved to tears. It was a fantastic summer of hard work. I grew as an individual.

I became more knowledgeable in all of my skills; even though I felt I was going to fall apart at times because I was on over drive. I made it. I was fine.

I decided to take the next three weeks off from all of my training. I needed everything to sink into my mind and review all the information. I was still working at the family restaurant and teaching dancing, but didn't need a break from that because I still needed money to continue training in a few weeks. I just needed a mental break from the summer before I went mental.

During my few week hiatus I attended more auditions for print ads, film and TV because I had more spare time and I was going online and applying to other theatre companies all across Canada. I also had another bright idea, okay, I am sure by this point you're wondering to yourself, "Wow this guy is full of bright ideas."

Okay, I know with a bit of a sarcastic tone accompanied by some laughter, but hey, I am here to entertain you. I applied to cruise lines for just about every position I thought I would like. I applied as a singer, dancer, dance host, activities staff for young children and adults; I applied to most of the largest cruise lines in the world. I was keeping busy and trying to move ahead even though I was on a break. I know it doesn't sound like I was on break, but believe me, I was enjoying this time off and having a good time with friends and cousins that I needed to catch up with because of my busy summer time.

BACK TO BUSINESS

SEPTEMBER 2013

It was back to business. I had my break and started to train in all my fields of passion at about the second week of the month. Then, I got a phone call from my cousin Toula in Toronto to tell me Nia Vardalos was going to be interviewed on the *George Stroumboulopoulos Show* (a night time talk show with CBC in Toronto).

She suggested I go online and get tickets and I possibly could meet her. She knew my plan. I guess telling people what I am doing helps, because they can be on the lookout for any clues to help me. I went online to get tickets and couldn't figure it out, it wasn't as easy as it was supposed to be. I tried several times and couldn't get it. Okay, I know what you're thinking. I am a little computer slow. I am so computer slow it's not even funny. I try my best with technology, it's just not for me and it frustrates me to no end.

Toula called again a few days later because my cousin knows how I am with computers and asked, "Did you get the tickets yet?"

I said, "No." She wasn't surprised and laughed. I asked her if she could do it for me and she kindly did. I was very thankful for this favour because I was going to see Nia Vardalos. I thought here is my second chance to finally get my resume to her. I was ecstatic as usual, jumping for joy inside and fireworks of happiness going off in my head.

The show was taped in the studio at the end of the month. I walked into the CBC Studios downtown Toronto around 2pm. I approached the information desk and asked where I go for the show. The show is taped in the afternoons and airs at 11:30pm.

I was directed to wait in a long hallway which appeared to have 50-foot ceilings where there was a line-up of people waiting. The taping was at 3pm. I like to be early in everything I do, from auditions, to work just in case of traffic or any other situation that may occur on the way.

There was a very small museum at the end of the hallway. This is where I spent the next 45 minutes. There were microphones from the past 60 years until today; there was a write up about Mr. Dress Up that brought back childhood memories of this fantastic kids' show and they had a collection of items: life size car doors, house doors and drums just to name a few. On his show and other shows these items would make the sound of a car door opening and closing, same for the house door and the drums for maybe the sound of thunder. All these articles were placed in a room off the set during the show and used as needed; whereas, today all these sounds are programmed on a computer to use at the tip of our fingers. It's amazing how technology has advanced. At about 2:45pm I slowly made my way back to the waiting area for the show.

A lady came to our group of about 80 people and took us to one of the upper levels of the building where the taping would take place. We were told to use the washroom before the taping began. We were there for three hours and we weren't allowed to get up to use the washroom. We had to stay in our seats because they tape a few different interviews and need the audience to stay still.

I thought to myself, good God, I feel like a kid in primary school being told we couldn't move during an assembly and had to stay with our legs crossed and hands in our laps. Well, my next thought was how on earth was I going to get close enough to hand my resume to Nia if we had to sit down and couldn't move a muscle? I didn't panic. I mean these people were on a mission and had a show to do, but I was on a mission too. I had a dream to fulfill.

We all sat down and the show started. There were various people interviewed, I didn't have a clue who they were and I didn't even remember who they were after the show was done. Finally, Nia Vardalos came out. She wore a black dress with high platform shoes and decorated in the latest jewellery trend. She walked on stage with a bright bubbly smile and was greeted with a warm applause. She had a glow of happiness accompanied by a beautiful smile when she walked out and sat down in the chair to be interviewed. She was interviewed on her book *Instant Mom* where she talks about adopting her little girl, her ups and downs about wanting to be a mother so bad and her career in show business. It's a fantastic and animated book. She puts a positive twist on everything, even her hardships. I highly recommend reading it; she offers information on adoption at the back of her book, which is helpful for people wanting to adopt a child.

The interview started and she spoke about how *My Big Fat Greek Wedding* changed her life. People always said how down to earth she is and she really is. The life she worked so hard for didn't go to her head. She was a grounded individual and so real.

Throughout this interview I was trying to figure out how I was going to give her my resume because we couldn't move from our seats. I had my resume and my headshots folded into a pocket size envelope ready to hand to her at any time. I kept pondering how on earth I was going to give it to her? I had another bright idea. Well, I know she's funny and I thought what if I throw it at her as she was leaving off stage and yell, "Catch." I hope you're laughing because I am. Then, I thought to myself that was a dumb idea because then I would get into trouble, probably big trouble.

Her interview was coming to an end and I was starting to give up. I knew we weren't allowed to stand up and move around. The CBC employees had work to do and I didn't want to look like some crazy person trying to get attention and be a disruption that could possibly get me into trouble. The interview was done. She walked off stage and my soul started to sink. I started to clap with the rest of the audience and I was melting down having missed an opportunity to hand her my resume. My eyes started to well up and there was nothing I could do. As the crew was preparing for their next scene, she came charging through the doors again. This time with plates of birthday cake! It was her birthday and there was a cake for her in the back and she came out to share it with the audience.

Instantly, I became really happy again. She was giving out cake, talking to the audience and being social with everybody. She was on the other side of the room. The studio people weren't impressed, but she was talking to her fans. Which I thought was fantastic. I said to myself, she must be coming over here at some point to chat with my side of the room. She left the room again and I thought to myself, it's done she's not coming back. I was having a roller coaster of feelings. There goes my opportunity again. I sat in my chair looking across the room with disappointment.

All of a sudden she came back with plates of cake again. I was instantly happy again. I was praying to my lucky stars that she would come and give me a piece of cake, then I could hand her my resume. All of a sudden she came to me, I was sitting in the front row and she gave me a piece of cake. I was in shock and froze. She was standing in front of me and I couldn't even spit up the word boo, even if I was asked to do so. My prayers were answered and I just looked in awe at her like a child. She offered me a piece of cake and I said, "No thank you."

She then asked, "You don't like cake?"

I said, "No." She smiled and gave it to the girl next to me.

I couldn't believe I just choked on the opportunity to exchange cake for resume. She started to talk to people about five chairs away from me and I finally had my Eureka moment. I thought it's time to give her my resume, she was close again and my luck couldn't get any better. I bent down, put my hand under my chair to get my pocket-sized resume, but the CBC staff pulled her away because she was holding them up and they wanted to start the next shoot. She was there for about 15 minutes extra and I blew it! I got nervous and I blew it! She was right in front of me with cake and I just blew it! I was so disappointed in myself.

We had to stay glued to our seats for about another 30 minutes and couldn't move. The show was finally done. I approached an employee and asked if I could hand my resume to Nia Vardalos. I was told the stars leave the building once their interview was over.

I was so disappointed in myself. One thing I recommend here is that you can't let your emotions get the best of you like I did. I froze up and lost the opportunity. You have to stay calm and be collected; approach the situation as best as possible even though your heart is racing with nervousness. I left the building trying to contain my emotions. I walked out of the building and down the street to a sub shop and stuffed my face. Then I walked back to my car, got in, closed the door and began to cry like a five-year-old child wanting his mother because he had just fallen off his bike. I know, I'm a 34-year-old pathetic 230-pound-man (yes I know I could stand to lose a few pounds) crying in his car like a child. I was so disappointed that I missed my chance. Once I was done, I drove home, told my close friends and they were disappointed for me too.

The next day I got up and started searching again for a book signing of some type. I figured she had to have some type of book signing, somewhere, some place. I found out she had a signing in Worchester, just west of Boston. You ask where? You got it, yes that's right, it's a Greek community and the signing was to be held at Saint Spyridon Greek Orthodox church on November 5th.

I thought to myself, perfect, it was going to be easier to approach her there than at the CBC studios. The signing would be full of Greek people and it would be a more relaxed atmosphere. It was an eight-hour drive, but I didn't care. I had gone half way across the world by plane to chase a dream, what's an eight-hour drive? I called the church and booked a few tickets. I found the community's Facebook page, found the address and sent them a money order for the tickets. I was happy once again and on a mission.

FOR REAL!

OCTOBER 2013

After a long day of teaching dancing I came home on a Sunday night and turned on the TV. I was flipping through station after station and there was nothing of interest to watch on any English channel, so I opted to see what was on the three Greek channels we have at home via satellite. The first two channels had nothing on that I liked so I tried the third which is named Ant1.

Dancing with the Stars in Greece was on and I thought I would watch the re-run. I watched closer and I noticed the main hostess was a different woman and that the judging panel was different too. It wasn't the re-run of season three; it was the premiere of season four.

I kept watching to make sure. It was season four and it had different professional dancers and different stars. I was crushed. My heart sank and I was so disappointed in what I was watching. The director told me I would get a phone call for season four. I didn't get that phone call. I was happy to see some of the professional dancers I knew because they were fantastic. I was disappointed. He did tell me last year when we spoke that the dancer and the star needed to look nice together, so maybe I wasn't the right fit for this season and I may be the right fit for the next season. I was holding on to that hope and not thinking I had been forgotten. I was working so hard and wasn't going to entertain the thought of giving up. It just wasn't an option for me no matter how upset I felt. I needed to keep going forward and not look back.

LET'S DO IT AGAIN!

NOVEMBER 2013

On Monday the 4th of November I woke up around 9am, got ready and got into my car for my eight- hour journey to Worcester, Massachusetts. I double-checked to make sure I had my resume, my passport and a nice change of clothes for the book signing.

I hopped in my car, filled my tank with gas and drove singing the songs that were on the radio. I was more relaxed at this point because I knew Nia Vardalos' book signing was going to be more relaxed than at the CBC studios, at least I was hoping so. I had a gut feeling it would be easier to speak with her. There weren't going to be people trying to film several shows. She was going to give a talk and sign her books. I was thinking, don't get nervous this time, if she offers me a piece of cake, take it and then give her my resume.

I arrived at the hotel around 6pm, having stopped a few times on the way to fill up for gas. I checked into my hotel room, had a bite to eat at a local restaurant accompanied by a few beers and just relaxed for the evening.

The following morning I got up at 11am and the first thing I did when I got out of bed was make sure my resume and headshots were in my backpack. I had prepared a nice resume package for her. I put my resume, headshots; my singing and dancing material (my YouTube links of singing and dancing) on a flash drive and I also prepared a hard copy of everything too. I wanted to make sure she had all my information in all types of media possible. I made sure all my contact information was on every piece of paper. The book signing was at 5pm. It was noon and I wanted to find the location so I wouldn't be late. I got in my car and about 15 minutes later I found St. Spyridon Greek Orthodox church and community center.

Now that I found the church and was acquainted with the area, I drove to a small neighbourhood restaurant and had some lunch. While eating I calmed myself down and tried not to get nervous and miss another opportunity to hand in my resume. I had plenty of time to kill. After sitting in the restaurant for quite some time I waited for 5pm to roll around. I got to the community center at around 2:30pm and I saw it was open.

I approached one of the event organizers; her name was Amy. I told her I was from Canada. I asked if I could park my car in the parking lot before the event and she kindly said yes. Now, I was here early, very early, so I walked around the neighbourhood for the next few hours taking pictures of old buildings and new ones. It was a beautiful little town.

As I was wandering around, I stumbled upon a small museum. It was a three-room museum and I discovered the city was settled in 1713. That explains the mixture of beautiful new and old architecture throughout the town. After my visit, I continued to walk around the area and I stopped to have a bagel. It was 4pm and I was starting to get hungry. The nice sales girl gave me a bag of bagels as I left because it was nearing the end of their day and they were about to close, I left with a dozen bagels.

It was now 4:30pm and I made my way to the church and got there about ten minutes later. I went in, got my ticket, purchased three books and found my designated seat. There were about 250 seats. At one end of the room was wine and snacks, so I helped myself. By this time my heart was pounding with excitement. Finally, I was going to meet her and give her my resume. I just kept saying to myself don't ruin it this time. I just had to stay calm and not get nervous. It was supposed to start at 5pm. It was now well after 5pm, but hey we're Greek and we never start anything on time. Father Dean came in, read an opening prayer and said a few words to everyone and then presented a gift to Nia on behalf of the Greek community.

Nia was greeted with a warm applause. She greeted everybody and started talking about her book. She is an animated, friendly and all around warm individual. She connected with the audience as she spoke about her ups and downs in show business and her long awaited process of wanting to be a mother.

As I was listening, I discovered through her talk that she too was having a very hard time getting work in show business. I wasn't happy at the fact that she was struggling, but at the simple fact that I wasn't the only one in this business having a hard time and listening to her story gave me some hope again.

It was about 6:30pm when her presentation was over. People came up row-by-row to get their book signed and have a photo taken with her too. She was friendly with everybody, greeting them with a warm smile and a handshake. Some people brought her small gifts and this young couple brought her a huge bundt cake wrapped in purple cellophane, it was the size of a car tire! It was nice to see people so happy to see her and have her autograph their books.

I made sure I was going to be the last person in line, so I just lingered around. Well, I was at the wine and snack table at the back of the hall stuffing my face and having a few big cups of wine to calm myself down because I was a little bit nervous. I didn't want to ruin it again. I thought I better go back to my seat and stop drinking wine before I get tipsy and then when I see her I would be laughing from the happy juice.

The line was still long and I was chatting up with various people and telling them why I was here. They were amazed that I came from so far just to talk to somebody for a few minutes to give them a resume. I thought I better get in line now, the line was getting shorter so I made my way to the end. There were these two young girls in front of me, they were sisters and in their early 20s and we just started chatting. I was telling them my story and they thought it was the coolest thing.

They proceeded to say, "Let us be the first people to have your autograph!" So I signed the back of Nia Vardalos book for them. I was delighted and very flattered. It was the coolest thing to sign my name for somebody else and I thought in my head, "Wow I would love to do this again."

The line was getting shorter and shorter. The hall had less and less people. I was getting closer and closer to Nia Vardalos and trying to stay relaxed.

I looked at my watch and it was 8:40pm. There were about five people in front of me in line and Nia said with a smile, "Wow guys thanks for waiting for me."

As the other people were getting theirs books signed, a woman from the organizing committee said to me, "Are you the guy that drove eight hours to come here?"

I said, "Yes."

She answered, "Good for you!"

Nia heard and her head popped up from signing because at this point I was only about ten feet away from her and she said, "Wow!"

My time was here, I was the last one in line and my heart was racing. I smiled as I approached her and tried to conceal my nervousness. I walked up to her and she greeted me with a smile and said, "Wow, thanks for coming. That is so sweet of you and thanks for coming so far to see me."

I gave her my three books and she laughed with delight and shook my hand.

I said, "I drove eight hours from Hamilton, Ontario, Canada to speak with you. Can I have two minutes of your time?"

She smiled and answered, "Yes."

At this point I was trying not to be nervous and trying to stay clam so I wouldn't choke again. I took a small breath and said, "I am a singer, dancer, actor and I want to work with you." She smiled and I continued, "I have my resume, head shots and videos for you in various forms in this envelope."

She smiled with delight and accepted it with care and honour. She told me she looks at and keeps everybody's resume on file. She added, "It's nice to see our Greek names in show business and we need more of them!"

Instantly, I had a happy dance of joy going on inside of my soul. I told her I was trying my best to give her my resume for a long time now.

I then proceeded to ask her, "Were your parents at the Greek Orthodox church in Hamilton for this past Pascha (Easter)?"

She smiled and said, "Yes."

Then I proceeded to tell her I was trying to give her my resume when she was on the *George Strombolopoulos Show*. She was touched. I was nervous throughout these two minutes and I was focused on trying to tell her everything I could and my nervousness got the best of me because I wanted to tell her something else and I just went blank.

I said, "I had something else I wanted to tell you and I forgot!" So I reiterated, "I really want to work with you at some point." Hoping that would trigger what I wanted to say, it didn't, so I wrapped it up and said, "Thank you so, so, so much for taking my resume and letting me chat with you, I really appreciate it."

She said, "You're welcome." And gave me a hug. We got our photo taken, as did everybody else, and she added again, "Tasos, thank you so much for coming down."

As I was going back to my chair to get my backpack and my coat, I happily called out, "Wait! I remember what I wanted to tell you, can I tell you?"

She smiled and said, "Yes."

I said, "My resume, it's not just my acting resume it's my life resume and everything I have done up until this point in my life."

She said, "Good for you because it lets me know more about who you are."

She started to gather up her belongings and chatting with the organizers. I was just lingering in the back where the snacks and wine were pretending to send text messages on my cell phone keeping an eye out because I didn't want her to forget my resume package.

After a few minutes she had all her belongings and she held my resume package in her arms like a book. I counted to ten in my head after she went through the door just so I didn't look like that much of a weirdo. I exited the same door to go to my car, she was pleasantly chatting and greeting the organizers standing next to a nice black limousine. I walked by and said a general thank you and good night to everyone standing outside. I didn't want to overdo it and look like a freak, but Nia turned to me as she was getting into the limo and pleasantly said with a smile, "Taso thank you again for coming down and drive home safely."

I replied, "Thank you for everything, I really appreciate it." I was so excited, she called me by my name, now we're friends (well not really ha, ha, ha). I was just excited that now she knew me by name and hopefully she won't forget who I am. Okay, so I am a little pathetic, but you would be too after working so hard to get where you want wouldn't you?

She got in the limo with my resume package in her arms and then departed as I was walking back to my car. I was so happy with how things went. It went better than I expected. I had butterflies of happiness going around in my stomach and I could have screamed with joy. She had my resume, knew my name and was going to learn more about me when she reads everything.

I sat in my car for a few minutes with a smile on my face looking out the window and envisioning more of my dream coming to life. I drove back to my hotel where I called my friends

Virginia, Diana and Mark and had a three way conversation with them. They were hanging out together and I told them all about this evening, they were really happy for me. I got up the next day at about 10am, got ready, packed, checked out and drove eight hours back home feeling sheer satisfaction and delight.

IT'S NOT OVER, IT'S JUST THE BEGINNING

JANUARY 2014

It's been a roller coaster of emotions and a colossal amount of hard work on my journey to this point: happiness and tears. I've worked hard at various dance studios and finding the best place for me to work. I have been travelling all over the world meeting directors, handing my resume to them and going to auditions everywhere. I have done my best trying to get a dance partner and at the same time certifying myself in as many dance styles and levels possible. I have worked hard at dancing, singing, acting, fire poi and the killer aerial silks. I have done my best to help my parents out at our family restaurant on the weekends. I have obtained a BA in Classics (Greek and Roman Archaeology), a certificate in world archaeology and a certificate in photography too. I have managed to keep my archaeology resume updated by doing one project a year since I graduated (from excavations to photographing of artefacts) and I have photographed weddings and other events too. I have made sure all my resumes are current and up to date. I have poured my life and soul into my dreams, I have spent about $100,000 dollars in education, I have made myself quite knowledgeable in all my fields over the past 15 years and I'm still learning every day in all of them.

I haven't been successful in finding a new dance partner, but I have been working with a very advanced student on the weekends from the Ciao Bella Dance Studio in Woodbridge. Her name is Patti Easson and we have become great friends too. She is talented, a great dancer, a great friend and I have become a better dancer because of her.

It's been killer hard listening to people tell me I'm not good enough, "You don't dance well, you don't sing well, you don't act well ..." And then being told that I do sing, dance and act well, only to find myself going nuts: one coach praises you and another disagrees with what was said.

I enjoy watching the *Ellen DeGeneres Show*; she is an inspiration. She's an individual that turns negatives into positives and has become a successful person. She enjoys happy times with her guests and audiences. I like her happy way of life and I use it as part of my daily life too. An episode of her show is uplifting if I am having a down day. I've also found Oprah's *Program of Life Classes* a great help too and listening to her advice can be helpful too. Let's not forget the *Marilyn Denis Show* too, having a cup of Greek coffee with her is wonderful in the mornings.

I've been told to stay in the business by coaches because I am a triple threat: a singer, dancer and actor. I am stronger and willing to stick it out because I really want to fulfill my passion, my dream. I keep reinventing myself -that is the key to moving forward.

Everybody has an opinion. People are entitled to their opinion, but my advice is to be as strong as you can be. It can be hard to handle at times. I have been called stupid, dumb, a loser and told to stop dreaming. I have been told to get a real job. I have been called lazy. I have been told I have no focus. I have been told in so many words (because I haven't been following the crowd) that I am an outcast and missing out on life. I have been told I have been wasting my time. I have been told I don't listen because I don't take advice that I feel is not conducive to my lifestyle. I have been told I think everything is easy in life and that I take the easy way out. If I did think that, I wouldn't be chasing my dream. I would just get a job and forget my dream. I have been told I should have a deadline. I don't have a deadline, I feel the need to keep going and I will, this is how bad I want success. Dreams don't have deadlines. It's all based on feelings. I feel the need to keep going.

If I feel the need to stop, I will and it will be based on the feeling to stop, which will be a thought and happy decision, not on a deadline. And by who? By people I feel I know well, who know me and are close to me. Stranger's voices don't bother me, it's the voices I know that bother me. I have learned to deal with them too. It's been hard because when you don't follow the crowd people start to pass judgment. It's really hard, I mean really hard at times, but you have to learn to ignore it or it will deter you from moving forward. If you pay attention to all the negative situations and give them power then you will never move forward because you will spend all your time dealing with that instead of moving forward. Don't judge others; look at yourself first before you make judgement of others.

What do I want? I love archaeology and I will stay in it forever. I love the fact that I do one project a year for a few weeks. I want to be on stage and film as a singer, dancer and actor. It's my dream and I want to fulfill it. I love what I do. I feel alive when I do it and I want to inspire you to find your passion.

I want my dream to motivate you to get up and chase whatever dream you have. I am not telling you to do what I am doing, but if you want to, then all the power to you. I want to be your inspiration. I want you to find something you truly want out of life. I truly love what I do and I want people to feel the same way I do. I want my story to inspire you to be happy, to find happiness within your soul. What do you want out of life? How can you get it? Anything is possible with hard, hard work and perseverance. It's not easy, but it can happen.

I am not in competition with anybody. I just want to be me. I am not striving to be better than the person beside me. I learn from the talented people around me and don't push them away. I am striving to make myself a better person, to get the most out of life and out of my crafts and skills. I am at peace with myself; therefore, I am free to move forward and conquer my dreams.

Printed in Canada